Planting The Seeds

Poetry, Stories and Prayers

By Abby Wynne

Other Books by Abby Wynne

Energy Healing for Everyone
Spiritual Tips for Enlightenment
Energy Healing Made Easy
How to Be Well
The Book of Healing Affirmations
Heal your Inner Wounds

and
The One Day at a Time Diary

ABBY WYNNE

Planting The Seeds
Poetry, Stories and Prayers

Copyright © Abby Wynne 2020
ISBN 978-1-9163627-0-3

First published 2020 by Praxis Publishing
www.praxispublishing.ie

PRAXIS
PUBLISHING

LEGAL NOTICE

All rights reserved. No part of this book may be reproduced, stored in a retrieval system, or transmitted in any form, or by any means, electronic,
mechanical, photocopying, recording or otherwise, without prior written permission from Praxis Publishing, except in the case of brief quotations embodied in critical reviews and certain other non-commercial uses permitted by copyright law. Requests to publish work from this book must be sent to Praxis Publishing via their website www.praxispublishing.ie

I dedicate this book to the land of Ireland

*for every atom that belongs to me
is an atom that belongs to you*

Acknowledgements

Thanks to my good friend and editor Robert Mohr for his wise words and kind editing hand. Thanks to my daughter Megan Wynne for the beautiful illustrations which decorate the interior, and the exterior. Thanks must go to Sofia Gazarian for putting Megan's illustrations together and creating a remarkable cover. I'd also like to thank Stephen Brown for his invaluable help and support over the years as my work has grown and transformed.

These poems, stories and prayers have been many years in the making. I acknowledge my own journey, my younger self, and the self I am becoming. I honour both the darkness and light on my path. For the path always knows where it is going, it is only us that doubt ourselves along the way.

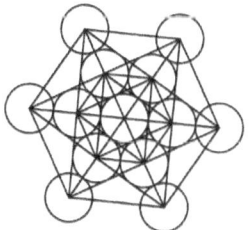

There is healing in these words

If you seek to find it, you must slow down into the moment softly
and open your heart to receive it.

The wisdom, well, that's within you already.

Table Of Contents

Acknowledgements 7

Opening Prayer 17

Ignorance Is Bliss 19

Soul Mate 21

Three Sides To Every Story 23

A Prayer For Difficult People 25

Ursula's Regret 29

Evil Exists 33

Horrible 35

Stressful 37

The Magical Girl 41

Uncommon Sense 45

Song Of Woman 1 47

Handbags 51

A Prayer To Amplify Love 53

Blowing A Fuse 55

Slow Down 63

A Tree Story 65

Françoise Et Papa 71

I Cut Myself 85

Be With It 89

A Prayer To Let Love In	91
Box	93
The Work	95
Song Of Woman 2	97
Depression	103
The Strength Of Cranes	105
Cat	107
Prince Sannu	109
Growth Hurts	131
A Prayer For Healing	133
Pink Ribbons	135
We Are Getting Stronger	139
Master Of Time	141
Enlightenment	143
The Magical Boy	145
Tribute To Roethke	173
A Prayer For Soul Retrieval	175
Quilt	177
Who Am I?	179
Intention To Heal	183
Always Here Be Magic	185
The Rescue	187
Mission Almost Impossible	201

A Prayer Of Gratitude	203
Quench	205
Growing Up	209
Song Of Woman 3	211
In Stillness	215
Maybe The World Isn't Broken	217
Elixir Transformangelico	219
Don't Give Up	235
Juniper	237
A Prayer To Open Sacred Space	243
About The Author	247

Spiritual Truths

or
Things that your Mother never told you

or
Things that you may not be ready to stomach just yet

Planting seeds my dear...
don't mind me,
I'm just planting the seeds.....

Opening Prayer

Dear God,

Please help me remove my blocks to love.
Help me reach deeply into my heart and send the healing there.
Help me see past old hurts and give me the strength to forgive the unforgivable.
Teach me how to forgive myself.
Show me how to love everyone.
Even the most irritating people deserve to be loved.
Let me feel your love come through me and into them.

Dear God,

I am of service to you
Use me as thy wand and point me in the direction you wish me to turn.
Those that seek me shall know your grace and mercy.
And when I am alone, I am never lonely,
as you reside within me always and forever.

And so it is.

Ignorance Is Bliss

Why do human beings write about the beginning of the world?
This stubborn insistence they have upon knowing how all was made?
And why do people try to give God a name?
Or fathom the depths from whence he came?

What if it was all created a split second ago, exactly as it is right now?
And you, the centre of it with your memory intact?

What if there was no "in the beginning"? Perhaps it started at the end, or in the middle?

Be with the not knowing
then appreciate the now moment all the more.

We are many stories many lifetimes all happening
in different dimensions at the same time,
and even in our complexity
there's no possibility the human mind could put the puzzle together when we are but insects compared
to the continent of a single piece
made for the hands of another being
who could accidentally squash us while reaching for the sugar,
as they drink their tea and read the paper in a shaft of sunlight on a Sunday morning.

Soul Mate

This person she depends on,
the one she calls "soulmate",
does she feed from them?
Does she greedily feast on the beauty of their life
force because she's too lazy to replenish her own?

This "soulmate" of hers....
Are they free to grow in their own way in their own
time without her?
Are they 'allowed' to out-grow her?
Then what would she do?

Closed hand captures the bird that longs to fly
"But we are soulmates" she says as she tightens her
fist, suffocating and strangling the very one that loves
her most of all.

Three Sides To Every Story

Goldilocks was oh so pretty yet she took and broke things that were not hers.
Those "big scary" bears took her in and forgave her anyway.

Appearances are deceiving.
Don't judge a book,
don't judge a person by how they look

That 85-year-old man beside you? He is on his first incarnation,
he didn't learn his lessons; he's coming back to experience a harsher world to squeeze and ring him out and open his heart.
That baby gurgling in its sleep is 3750 years old and brings hard earned compassion and kindness in her eyes to everyone she meets.

Your neighbours, you know the ones you're jealous of with the big fancy car and the holidays and the huge salary? They're on their holiday life, a break where they can assimilate and equilibrate all of the pain they experienced in their 10 previous lives in chains of slavery and bondage.

And the soulmate you want to go on your spiritual journey with?
He needs need another 300 years of preparation to catch up with you.

A Prayer For Difficult People

We are all sisters and brothers to each other. Please help me see everyone as family; those that are my blood relations, those that are my friends and those that I haven't met yet.

Let me open my heart to all whether I like them, understand them, or not. Because we are all divine beings having a human existence.

We are all struggling with our life situation, our personalities, our limiting beliefs and our eccentricities. I step away from others and now I see them in a different light.

I no longer wish to live in fear of the other. I step away from fear. Now is the time for love. I give permission to let the love into my own heart and allow it to spill out from me and around me and into the atmosphere around me.

I offer pure unconditional love to anyone who needs it without expectation or desire for recognition or award.

I no longer need to compromise myself for someone else's small personality. I honour my boundaries and the boundaries of others. When I let love into my heart I expand and I dissolve away and all there is, is love.

I can forgive the others but I do not need to forget. I can love them but I can do it from over here. I close the business between us and I do not owe them anything.

What they have done or not done, who they are and who they pretend to be, the choices that they have made and how they live their life is between them and God.

I wish them well. I wish them happiness and joy. I wish they may find love in their hearts so they can also bring more love into the world. And now I let them go.

Amen

Ursula's Regret

Ursula swept the floor of her cave and put her magical tools back into the chest. "That girl really is much too much trouble for what she is worth", she thought and shook her head as she picked a piece of dirt off of the seal from one of her magical potions.

"Imagine, wanting to give up all of her freedom – for what? A human? And a man at that! Shocking," she said, tut tut tutting as she reorganised the jars on her shelf, almost tripping over Flotsam as he skittered across the floor to get out from under her tail. He took one look at Jetsam and nodded, both congers drifted towards the mouth of the cave, and with a whoosh, they both disappeared out into the vastness of the sea.

"Giving it all away for a man," muttered Ursula under her breath for about the seventh time. "Does she not know who she is?? A princess of the sea, no less, and yet...," she said out loud with exasperation, "What a stupid girl. Stupid stupid stupid." With a lower voice, she muttered down to the floor, "I shouldn't have given her up."

Ursula poured herself a large gin and flopped down on her most comfortable chair. A tear formed in her left eye. She shook her head again and took a drink of gin.

"And there I was, thinking that if I asked her for the most precious thing she owned, her voice, she'd see how crazy she was, and realise her stupidity, but no. No no no. And then I had no choice but to take it. Isn't that right Flotsam? I have my reputation to maintain." Ursula turned around to look for her loyal friend "Flotsam? Jetsam? Where are you? Arghhhh!" She threw the empty gin bottle against the wall and a current swept it away before it had a chance to smash itself against the cave. She sunk down again into her chair, another tear forming, this time in the right eye. "Would it have been any different at all if I had kept the child?"

Ursula cast her mind back to that magical day with King Neptune, the picnic on the algal fields, the way he looked at her, she was beautiful then, yes, even her true face was fresh and full of hope. They had made love, spontaneously, not worrying or wondering about anything but their closeness, and when they departed, she was with child.

He of course rejected her out of hand, straight away, she wasn't from royal stock, no, not Ursula. Her mother had been shunned out of the neighbourhood and forced to live a life of solitude, Ursula used to sneak away and spend moments daydreaming on the algal fields, and that's where she met King Neptune. Of course, he was a prince then, and Ursula, not knowing much about the township or the townspeople, didn't know he was a royal. To her, he was just the most beautiful merman she had ever seen.

With a sigh, she brought her awareness back to where she was, right now, empty gin glass in hand and a conundrum in her heart – what to do with this child who had, to all intents and purposes, lost her right little mind. She stood up and went to the mirror on the wall, and looked at her reflection deep, and hard. Perhaps she could change herself, woo this new prince away from Ariel so that Ariel would see how fickle he was, how he wasn't worth wasting her life on. What else was a mother to do?

Evil Exists

Evil is real.

You're kidding yourself if you think otherwise.
Evil draws you in, claws at you with hooks,
flesh and bone pinned and tangled
until line and sinker it's too late to leave it.

Yes, there's no such thing as an innocent babe if you
believe in incarnation.
Do we all really get a choice? Or to choose the
choices that we make?
Is choice the illusion of the entitled few?

For where Evil lurks there are only slaves
who toil
with quotas
(like car clampers).

They would feast on your Soul, pretty one, and they
would feast on you eagerly
if you don't run from here.

Horrible

Yes, it was horrible,
all of it
horrible.
Those horrible things that happened to you,
those past events, awful.

I say this with love in my heart.

But you will not find the beauty you lost by traipsing through memories of events that have already taken on a life of their own in your mind.
Your beauty goes where all beauty goes when evil is around.

And digging trenches, sinking your hands deep into the mud to look for buried treasure will not bring you anywhere closer to the truth.

Go looking in a boneyard and you will only find more bones.

You have mud under your fingernails. It poisons everything you touch. Clean your hands now.

Those therapists want only to try the latest technique they learned from YouTube.
Stirring the mud around and around by talking does not clear it.

You are nobody's guinea pig,
your lack of self-worth is temporary and attractive to
those who feed off vulnerability.

You cannot heal Spirit using the mind alone.

Come on a journey with me and find the pieces that
you lost,
and put the jigsaw puzzle of your beautiful Soul
back on the mantelpiece where it belongs.

Stressful

stress
eats
away
at
the
very
core
of
your
being

unplug yourself
from the stress of the world

go on, I dare you
like you unplug your phone or your computer
you have a plug
pull it out of the wall
pull it out of the fear matrix
you won't die from this I promise

the frazzled bits of you that are left
need time to
un
wind
and
relax

they will

if you
let
them

s
l
o
w

d
o
w
n

create
space
for
peace

create
space
for
sleep

create
space
for
that
marvellous
elixir
to
come

and
fill
you
up
and
heal
your
broken
pieces

it can't come in
if you're closed off to it

it's so much easier to just plug yourself back into
that fear channel
and feast on that adrenaline high

you burnt-out crisp of a thing
slim skeletal wisp of a thing
all that's left is crunchy bones and an empty pocket
aching for the very thing
that only you could give to yourself
if you open the door and let it in

The Magical Girl

Once upon a time a magical girl was born. Her family was delighted to see her, and she was delighted to see them, so delighted that her heart lit up so strongly, it almost blinded them. They were all surprised at how bright this girl could be and they didn't know what to do with her. So they loved her as best as they could, but they kept their distance from her, in case she hurt their eyes.

When the little girl was three she realised her family was afraid of her. They would shield their eyes when she came into the room, and they wouldn't give her those big strong hugs that a little girl needs. They were similar to those type of distance hugs that you would give to someone you didn't really know very well. The little girl became sad but she did not understand why. One day she was overwhelmed by her sadness and it flooded into her heart. Her heart got smaller, and as a result, her light shrank. But for some reason her family seemed to be happier with her like this, and they stopped shielding their eyes, and they even hugged her a little tighter over time, yet still not as tight as the little girl needed.

As time went by, the little girl grew and discovered things that she loved, and for a few moments she would forget her sadness and her heart would shine brightly again. Her father became angry at her when her light was too strong for him;

her mother would stop hugging her when she shone her light too brightly around her. As a way to deal with it, her family would give her chores to keep her busy. Soon she would become burdened by the work and her light would dim. Over time she eventually stopped looking for things to make her happy, and she stayed mostly sad, mostly heavy, and mostly dull.

When she went to school, the children were nice to her face but said she was strange behind her back. One afternoon one of the bigger girls came up to her and pulled her hair, spat in her face and told her that she was never to try to be friends with anyone. She said all the girls in the class were HER friends, and our little girl was not allowed to have even one friend. That made our girl even more upset, and unbeknownst to her, the very last spark of joy went out of her heart.

She walked with her head down. She forgot to tie her shoelaces. She did her homework and her household chores and spent the rest of the time looking out the window, not really doing anything at all. She didn't know why she was alive. She forgot about her light. The colours of her world were gone and she felt dead inside.

As she got older she went to another school, but she didn't even try to make friends there. She kept her head down, did her studying and came home, did her housework, and when she wasn't doing that, she looked out the window. There wasn't anything that interesting outside her window anyway. It was a plain garden with a single tree in the middle, a few rose bushes and some weeds. Her family was not really interested in gardening.

When she looked outside at the tree, she would blur her vision so that she couldn't really see it anymore. The tree looked fuzzy, like it was moving from side to side, and if she stared hard enough, it would almost disappear.

There was always a noise, like her mother calling her down for dinner, or to do the laundry, that would snap her back to her body and the tree would suddenly reappear. But each time she came back, she felt less and less like she was really here. She didn't know where she was. Perhaps she wasn't anywhere at all.

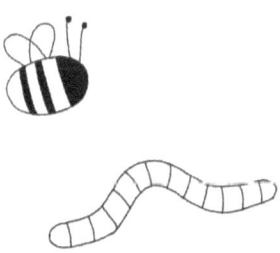

Uncommon Sense

Knowing when to stop
is a gift that many
have been born
without.

Song Of Woman 1

Every pore
breathing colours
passion
swallows body
consumes the Soul until
we disappear

An emotional drunk
I know not what I do
or what I say
or whom to
nor do I care

Unspoken need to be desired
every pore calls out
to be
kissed
held
loved

I carry grief in my back pocket
(the heart has many pockets)

Endless capacity for love and pain
endless need
for love
and pain

Emotional pockets to be filled

scares him
scars us
sacred

Oh Scarlet Heart if only you were not so demanding

I am woman

Strong
connected
to all things living or have once lived
now, past or
unfolding

I am woman
and I love

And other women
talking secrets on the street
behind each other's backs
lying
laying down on damp patches
not sacred

we go on
mostly alone

I am woman
and I bleed

fresh blood
red blood

dark blood
all colours blood

I clean it up
it's not appropriate

I am woman
vulnerable
open and
ashamed
"I'll never go that way again"
I do it anyway

I keep my pain
because its mine

Behold his naked virility
as he holds his manhood in pride
and pisses into the wind in full view
not needing reassurance
he has everything he needs right there
in his own hands

I am woman
gaping hole
gaping whole
needs to be filled

Standing tall now stand taller
when standing on a box
in six-inch stiletto heels asking for sex no strings
and something inside died

So fly away now, go now
You won't be let see those
silver threads connected from
my heart to your wings

I'll wait for your return
and in the meantime
I'll write an epic poem to be remembered by.

Handbags

New bag new beginning
Well, the leather is smooth
never been used and you can choose
to leave behind
some of the items you've been carrying around
perhaps a little too long
in the transfer

Is it a girl thing?
Brand new bag
like a personality change
big dark heavy or small and light
as I sip on not the best cup of coffee I've ever had
after spending once again too much money on
a brand new bag

Alanis you would not
have been so troubled if
you changed handbags
as often as I

A Prayer To Amplify Love

Dear God,

Please send a shockwave of love to the world to eliminate hate from the hearts of humanity and amplify compassion.

Encourage us to be the generous beings that we have the capacity to be.

May we come together and support each other and heal our environment.
May we eliminate oppression and injustice in the world.

May every child know that it is loved.
May every adult remember that it is a child of God.

I pray to you to amplify love
Amplify love, God
Amplify love.

Amen

Blowing A Fuse

What you see

They had been friends for over 20 years. He moved to London and as time went on, their contact was more and more infrequent. She had planned to go to London for an exhibition and he was in town, so they arranged to meet in a restaurant around the corner from his apartment for a few hours before she had to go to the airport to catch her flight home.

She was excited to see him and made haste to the appointed place and time. She was early, she took a table at the back and sat facing the door. Life walked past, London life so different to the town where she was from. So many different bodies, different shapes, skin colours, hair.... The one thing they did have in common was that they all looked like they were rushing somewhere. She ordered a coffee and waited, breathing, feeling herself slowing down and coming more and more into the room.

When the coffee arrived, she cradled it in her hands and tuned into other people's conversations. She put her phone aside. She had set an alarm for 3.30pm, plenty of time to get to the airport and avoid rush hour. It was 12noon and she allowed herself to relax for the first time in 2 days. It's funny how we must allow ourselves relax; you'd think it was something that would happen naturally.

However, we hold our bodies so tightly, in order to relax we do need to bring our awareness to the tightness and tell ourselves that it is okay to let it go.

The cafe was busy. The waitress had her pencil behind her ear as she cleared plates, and she was animated taking orders, making eye contact with everyone she spoke to. London didn't appear to have a set lunchtime or dinner time; people just showed up and ate, all the time. There were flowers on each table, music played on speakers softly and at the back there was a display case filled with cakes, pastries and macaroons that they claimed to have baked on the premises. The lighting was a combination of spotlights and florescent bulbs, just a little too bright.

He arrived, breathless, took off his coat and leant over the table to embrace her, his lips cold on her warm cheek. He looked like a stranger to her, his body language showed the distance that had grown between them.

"Hello darling," he said. "So good to see you - how long has it been?"

"Oh, about a year," she answered nonchalantly, the edges of her lips curling up into a subtle smile. She couldn't hold it back, she beamed at him, she was delighted to see him again.

He sat and smiled right back at her. "Shall we order something?"

As the food came, the conversation unfolded. "Do you remember that time...?"

"Oh yes! What about the time when...." They relaxed into it, the elements of the conversation were not as important as the heightened awareness of each other, the release of emotion, the renewing of the connection between them. As each remembered a time that was, the other recalled some detail that the first had forgotten. Like players putting together a familiar jigsaw puzzle, by the time the plates were taken away, they had laid out most of their relationship on some invisible etheric board, with only a few pieces missing.

"How was your exhibition?" he eventually asked.

"It could have gone better" she admitted. "I hadn't slept well, I stayed in an Air B&B the night before, but unfortunately the owner never said that she was having four guests and it was an open plan space."

"Oh dear."

"Yes, and I had just nodded off when another guest showed up at 1am in the morning. I felt very unsettled – there was too much going on in the house – it was as if I could hear what everyone was thinking, as well as feeling exposed since there was no door to close my room off from the others."

"I think it's time you upgrade your accommodation," he said "hotel rooms only from now on. I do hope you leave them a terribly bad review."

"Yes I will, and yes, you're absolutely right."

"You can't compromise yourself for the sake of spending a few less cents," he said. "It doesn't make any sense at all!"

They looked at each other and both said at the same time "That rhymes!" They laughed, together, free and loud and so happy to have reconnected. Suddenly, amongst all the laughter, all the lights went out in the cafe and the music stopped.

"What the hell?" She said and he laughed again.

"Looks like our laughter blew a fuse! This place probably could do with a good cleansing anyway!" They both continued to laugh.

"Time to leave?" She asked, checking her watch.

"Oh yes, most definitely. We don't want any further responsibility for their electrical problems!!"

They got up and the lights came back on. They put their coats on, split the bill and swiftly left the building. They hugged outside on the street and then went their separate ways, determined never to let the time apart go as long again.

What you don't see

That cafe had been there for many years, about as long as their friendship. If you were to visit the table where they had sat and let go of your focus of vision, blur your eyes and soften your frame of reference, you can peer underneath this reality, through and into the etheric layers that separate this reality from the other world. You would see the world of the fae, of myths and legends, of fairies and dragons. Perhaps once called the underworld, now revealed, not so much under but parallel, not veiled or far away, but here.

Right here, right now. Can you see it as you read these words? Some people can, they've been diagnosed as crazy, thrown into asylums or placed on medication.

Anyway, rewind back to the couple sitting at the table, the man and the woman enjoying their reunion. And look at that word, re-union. Union – connection, fusion, joining. In the etheric layers, their energy was conjoining, blurring, joyous and ecstatic, for their meeting created a pre-determined point in time and space that their human brains wouldn't understand or ever comprehend its significance.

For in his etheric field, he held the codes that she required for the next stage of her awakening. As they sipped coffee, their energy fields were mingling, and the codes were being transferred from him and into her. If you can see it in your imagination, it may look like different coloured lights, he with many colours, she with just a few, and as they connected and flowed in and out of each other, coloured lights in her energy lighting up to match his, and his pattern of lights sliding into her essence and switching off in him. A transferring of information, he no longer had to carry these codes, his contract with them was over.

And when they laughed the transfer was complete and there was such a burst of energy that the fuses in the cafe blew. Both he and she had a sense that they had something to do with the energy burst, but as nothing caught fire, it was quite acceptable to pay the bill and quietly leave without a fuss.

Of course, nobody would have been able to say exactly what was at fault. It's not like we typically blame people off the street for something as random as the blowing of a fuse.

Where did these codes come from? You may ask. And what are they?

Well, one year before this meeting, he had spent time in Mexico and was present in the high temple during the equinox when a shaft of light from the sun illuminated the cavern and shone on a specific hieroglyph that was engraved in the wall.

And in the etheric layer surrounding the hieroglyph, unbeknownst to everyone, was a very tiny packet of energy which had been embedded there, and which, of course was completely ignorant of the passing of time, or even the concept of time, because it was, well, asleep.

When the shaft of sunlight hit on that particular day when our designated person was present, this packet of energy which had been placed there when the temple had been built, activated. Meaning that it switched on its colourful lights and floated down from the wall and embedded itself into our friend's energy field.

He noticed after that event that he felt heavy in himself, like he was carrying about 10 lbs extra, and he couldn't shed that feeling of extra weight, no matter how hard he tried.

When they left the cafe that day, he noticed how light he was feeling, like that weight had just been lifted from him. He skipped back to his apartment, delighted to have seen her again, clear and free in his lightness.

Meanwhile, she took the tube to the airport to catch her plane home, all the while thinking that she should not have eaten that slice of chocolate cake. She felt very bloated and heavy. When would she ever learn to stop eating when she's full?

Slow Down

You move too fast
you might miss something
some thought
some packet of loose energy that is your next
awakening

A Tree Story

There is a tree that grows
deep roots in heavy, pungent soil
pulling earthy goodness up into the heart of it

Beating
beating
If you listen carefully to the
beating
you can hear its
double rhythm

Lovers entwined
Two hearts as one
imprisoned in the body of the tree

Many lifetimes many broken hearts over and over
and over again
And finally they become one
never to be separated again
An unfortunate wish, granted....

She awakes at starlight
gazing at his sleeping face under the moon
she adores him so

Love pouring forth from her heart into his,
watching him breathe while he sleeps
caressing him through nightmares

Longing to see his eyes open and tell him there is
nothing to forgive

He, waking only at the break of day,
at the moment when she drifts to sleep
longs to touch her, tell her how much he loves her,
how sorry he is
but afraid he will waken her
He can only watch her sleeping
remembers when he lost her, all the times he thinks
he broke her heart
and he is full of sorrows

1000 years the tree is growing
this blissful torture of separateness
yet togetherness
of love and hesitancy....

She can hear him thinking but cannot comfort him
and he can feel her love for him but he does not
believe it's deserved

So close...
almost touching...
feeling into the gap...
tension with no release....

Her tears feed the blossoms in the springtime and
his tears are the falling autumn leaves

Time passes

The landscape around them grows houses then
factories and towns
Fresh air turns thick with heavy fog pollution
The sound of chirping birds drowned out by traffic
noises
and the fairies have all flown away

Concrete surrounding the lovers tree
in a dead end of an estate
covered by graffiti, a favourite spot for drug addicts.

Still
their love prevails
Although never a single kiss had between them
Lips never touch
Yet such tenderness
Such outpouring of love, such devotion

All encompassing
surrounded by the emptiness and futility of
humanity
She holds onto him tighter
lest the pain surrounding them prise them apart
And then ... a miracle

Once in a thousand years
the sun and moon appear in the sky together!
In daylight she awakes to see his face
gazing down at hers

She smiles...
He realises...

And the sudden rapture they feel at the moment of
awareness
of their togetherness
Expands their hearts so greatly
the tree shatters
Lifting them completely out of their beautiful
prison.

The tree, now a hollow burnt out shell of a thing,
no longer a haven for children to ring-a-rosie
Or for teenagers to carve initials into.
The city that grew around them doesn't even notice
the death of the tree.
People walk by consumed by thoughts of poverty,
conflict or their next possession.

And above it all
the joyous freedom of the spirits entwined

He flows into her she flows into him
For every atom belonging to him is an atom
belonging to her.

The lovers reunited
Wounds heal and
all is forgiven
Enmeshed entangled in each other

Their blissful reunion
felt only by the wind
witnessed by Angels
and blessed by the sun and the moon.

Françoise Et Papa

The room was usually cold but she never noticed the cold. "Strong stock" Grandmamma said. When she used to pull on Grandmamma's skirts, her grandmamma would reach down her two hands and lift her up, carry her to the rocking chair, and settle her amongst her large thighs, then sing her songs of forests, magical nights and the moon. "Again again!" Françoise would shout with glee as her grandmother rocked her back and forth and sang. As she snuggled down in the warmth of the big woman's lap, Françoise would find her thumb moving towards her lips, and she would close her eyes, letting it into her mouth then slowly sucking, the comfort seeping into her bones, listening to grandmamma's voice, knowing that papa would be home soon. All was well and she was at peace.

She never knew her mother; she died during childbirth. There was just the one photograph and she was beautiful. Her mother was from Poland. She left her family to be with her father, so there was just Françoise, her father and her father's mother, Grandmamma.

Françoise and her father lived in the ground floor of a big, draughty house. It was a fine house once, filled with fine things; you could almost hear the laughter from the parties that were held there night after night. Dukes and duchesses, princes and princesses visited, but now the paint was peeling off the walls, the carpets were threadbare and only echoes of grandeur remained. Grandmamma inherited the house from her parents. She lived upstairs, and a lodger lived on the third floor.

Papa and Françoise shared a large downstairs room. It had old pine floorboards, some of them creaky, a few of them broken, some worn shiny from Françoise's dancing. There was a large bright window facing the street, a fireplace, a double bed, a small kitchenette and a piano.

Françoise and her father were very close, "Soul mates," Grandmamma said with a cluck in her throat and her eyes up to heaven. Françoise didn't understand what she meant, but she knew that somehow it was important, more special than just being dada and baba. Papa was her everything. When she looked at him, it was as if stars shone out of her eyes and her whole face lit up when he came into the room. "Papa! Papa!" she would shout and run to him, clinging onto his leg.

"My little limpet" he called her. Oh, those were happy days. He would play the piano, Françoise would put on a dancing show, and Grandmamma would clap her hands, throw her head back and laugh.

Once Françoise grew out of her little cot, it seemed natural for her to move into the bed with Papa. It was a matter of convenience more than anything else, for there was no room (and no money) for a second bed. In the early morning, the sun would creep into the room, creeping silently under Françoise's eyelids and rousing her from her slumber. In those delicious moments, she would look across at her papa as he slept beside her, one arm under his head, the other across his pillow, his chest rising and falling as he breathed. Her little body wriggled silently over to him, not to wake him but to look at his face, sometimes for hours, almost touching his cheek with her finger. She traced in the air the lines on his face, the lines around his eyes. She knew his face better than anything else in the world.

"Papa" she would whisper, "Je t'aime, Je t'aime tellement, plus que le soleil aime la lune, plus de la mer aime la terre," she whispered, words she didn't understand. They would catch her and she couldn't hold them in. When she spoke of her love, the words just came, like they were written on her Soul, as if she were reading a letter someone else had written. She had no choice, she had to let them out or she felt that she would die.

"Vous me faites avec tant d'amour et tout ce que je peux faire est de regarder sur votre visage et il y a tout cet amour en moi, je ne sais pas quoi faire. Je t'aime tellement. Je vous adore, mon roi, mon amour, mon papa." These words, they came into her and out of her, stronger at times than she ever thought she was herself. She was such a small being and yet felt so much love.... If she held it in, she couldn't breathe....

She tried, she tried one time, she actually stopped breathing, her heart pounding so hard that she almost turned blue, had to gasp for air.... She got such a fright and so did Papa. She couldn't fight it anymore, it became a ritual, every morning, it just was what it was. Sometimes it felt like she was dancing inside herself. She could see the love; she became pure love as if the love itself was jumping around the room outside of her, inside of her too, at the same time, filling her up, just because she was there and he existed. It was all that she knew.

In the moments when it would subside, he would awaken, opening his eyes. "Mon petite crampon," he would say to her and smile, and the love would crash in again, a tidal wave of it almost knocking her over. Next thing she knew she would awaken, and he'd be at the sink, his back to her and he brushing his teeth, humming a song and putting the kettle on the stove for his coffee. And then the day began.

That was how they lived. Joyful, love-filled days until the war came and took her papa away. She doesn't remember much about those early days, just vague recollection of smells, memories of the light, the flowers, Grandmamma's laughter and the piano. It had belonged to her great grandmamma, a beautiful grand piano fit for an orchestra. Her papa started teaching her when she was only 2, placing her little hands on his hands as he played. She felt the rhythm, and when she couldn't sit anymore, she would run and dance and he would continue to play. At 4 she was showing her talent. She sat on the stool, placed her hands on the keys herself and began to play.

It felt as if that part of her which escaped her during the morning ritual slowly came back solidly to her again with the music. She would play her scales diligently, seriously, because she knew it made him happy, and he would teach her all that he knew. Classical music, never local frolicking tunes, and as she grew so did her repertoire. She learned the pieces by heart and played with emotion.

The letter came one morning when she was 6, and a week later Papa was gone. Grandmamma moved downstairs, holding Françoise as she cried, all night restless in the bed, turning and tossing, pulling at her own hair, Grandmamma's voice eventually calming her, her thumb finding its way back into her mouth just as it did when she was a babe.

That first morning without Papa, the sun crept under her eyelids like it always did. But she felt nothing. No joy, no bliss, no love, just emptiness. It was a shock to her, like something in the world was out of place, something missing that was so huge, the very fabric of the world had a tear in it. Confused, she sat up in the bed, heart racing. "Papa!" she shouted but he was not there, just her grandmamma snoring in the bed beside her. Grandmamma shifted, then settled and started snoring again. Beginning to fret, she got up and paced around the room like a caged animal.

"My little one" said Grandmamma watching her, "it's alright, it will be okay, come back to bed my love." But she had to get outside; she couldn't stand it in the room without the comfort of her papa's love. She could not get back to bed and feel this emptiness tearing her apart.

"Come come Grandmamma. Let's go to the river," she said, tugging her grandmother out of the bed. Pulling on clothes, shoes, hats and scarves, they left in the early freezing dawn, walking on the cobblestones down the Rue D'Avignon, past the factory and onto the green and down to the rushing of the river. Under the canopy of trees, she felt she could breathe again. With the cold on her face, she felt the tears releasing. She sat and cried, and cried until she felt she could not cry anymore. The trees came to heal the ache in her heart, the wind blew the fear out from her stomach, the earth beneath her took all of the panic away.

And so it was for the first week. Instead of the rush of love in the mornings came a gap, then a remembering, then a panic. Some days were worse than others. Sheer panic cut her in two, and she was shaking so much, so deeply to the bone that only the trees, the river, the earth could relieve her pain. The days around it were slow as if time was crawling, and every hour felt like three. And then it was bedtime, brushing teeth, climbing into bed and Grandmamma singing her to sleep.

During the third week, there was a letter with her father's handwriting. She was filled with such joy, he was alive! But she was certain he had died! First more confusion, then she relaxed for a moment, and then the rush of love filled her heart, almost knocking her over, filling her all at once with a sweetness so fine, with flowers, with joy, such ecstasy and bliss she had to lie down, holding the letter to her chest, not opening it for hours lest the feeling pass.

When she eventually was able to open the letter, her hands shook., She was slow and deliberate so she wouldn't rip it, destroy any of the words. Every breath she breathed was a breath of his love. Her eyes took in every shape of each letter, the swirl of the writing, not just the words themselves, but the hand that wrote them, eating it up so she wouldn't miss a thing. It was short:

"My darling limpet, it is difficult here without you, cold and wet, and we are marching now. I have a heavy backpack, but in it I have the picture that you drew for me, and I remember our times together often. Are you playing the piano? Keep playing for me, every time you play I will hear you, even from so far away. My precious Françoise, I love you, I will be home to you before you know it. Do what Grandmamma says and be a good girl. Forever and always, Papa."

That was it. All of it. She read it again. She folded it and put it in the pocket of her dress. She touched it to make sure it was real. She took it out and read it again. Then folded it and put it back in her pocket. And again. He was alive. But why couldn't she feel that love, and then suddenly she felt it again? Was it she that shut him out? She let him into her heart once more, and the love came rushing back, softly, gently this time, but it was there.

She began to trust life again, the panic subsided and she did all her grandmamma asked of her. "I told you so, my little one, I told you. He will be home soon don't you worry. Now let's get this house in order. You're going back to school tomorrow". And as she was told to do all that her Grandmamma asked, she agreed.

The morning ritual began again. After some time, Grandmamma moved back upstairs to the comfort of her own room, and Françoise had the bed to herself. She enjoyed having the room to herself. She had learnt that when she let the love in, it came rushing in, and she didn't feel lonely anymore. She found herself waking up from sleep whispering the words once more. "J'taime J'taime J'taime, Je vous adore mon papa."

She opened her heart to let the honey sweetness in; it entered her body so gently, so softly and it was the same every morning. "J'taime tellement," she whispered to her papa in her slumber. Then sometimes she would remember he was gone to war – "Papa est parti..." – and the sadness came. She so badly wanted to be sad, really wanted to be missing him, grieving for him, but this honey sweetness kept rushing in, like waves on the beach. It refused to let her feel the heaviness of her grief. Anytime the grief came with the memory of him, it was as if gentle fingers scooped it out of her heart and filled her heart once more with love. She became frustrated, fighting the goodness, the sweetness of this love, wanting the pain of the sadness, but it wore her down, and she surrendered to it and let it consume her with bliss. Then it was time to get up for school, for the other, duller routines of her day, and the feelings of bliss would dissipate, and not return until the next day.

The rest of the day was difficult to get through. Food lost its taste. Only the piano brought her the solace she was looking for, and the morning ritual to look forward to.

"Come now my little one," said Grandmamma. "Your papa has enough to be worrying about without worrying about you too. Eat now, rest and grow. Do the things that little girls do and he will be back soon, back before you even know it."

Françoise expressed herself best through music, playing the heavy slow notes of Chopin, the restless scales of Bach, and the passion of Beethoven filled the ache in her heart. Thusly, the days went on. For months. No more letters came, and the one in her pocket was so crumpled from reading, the letters were hardly visible anymore and the paper worn thin.

And then, one day, her papa died in the war.

She just knew it. She felt it. Not the same as before, not the emptiness and nothingness of that first week, but the complete opposite of emptiness. Fullness. She was practising her Bach in the afternoon after another dull day at school when she felt him. Like a knocking on a door, the feeling of love, the flowers and the colours, crept into her awareness. She was startled that it came in the afternoon, and not in a passionate rush, but delicately. She stopped playing and closed her eyes. She felt her papa in the room. So close to her, so strong he was, it was as if he was really there in the room, wrapping his arms around her. She really felt him holding her.

"I'll never leave you again my sweet," she heard his voice in her mind, but his body was not there. Confusing but beautiful at the same time. She could almost smell him, it was different this time,

"Papa?" she said out loud and then felt a rush of air down her back, a cold shiver and all her hairs stood on end.

"Yes my darling, it is I, your papa."

He never left her since that day. All she longed for was to be alone, to let him into her heart, to feel the love between them, to hear his voice telling her how much he loved her, and she, telling him she was his little girl. Long into her teenage years, even long after Grandmamma passed away, she slept in the same bed that she had shared with her papa all those years ago, dreaming about him. Talking to him out loud more and more, playing her passion on the piano, the days went past. Men came to call, men asked her out, wanted to marry her (she was beautiful then as her mother was), but she had no interest in any of them. Lodgers came and went, their rent just enough to pay the bills.

No husband, no children entered her life, except for the ones that came for piano lessons. She would sit patiently beside them, pointing out their mistakes gently, praising them for their talents (which not many of them had), stretching them and growing them just as her papa did for her. In the evenings, she would light the fire, rock in the chair and remember her grandmamma. She found her thumb still moving towards her mouth, but she resisted for many years, until one day she gave in and found that comfort once again.

Time passed, and she became old. Tired. Less and less interested in this life. Françoise usually ignored the knocking on the door. The local children went through a phase of throwing eggs through the letterbox, laughing as they ran away, but once they knew they would not be chased, chastised or caught, it no longer was fun and they left her alone. One of the local women would bring bread, milk and eggs, sometimes cake. One in particular would make her tea and set the fire. One day she bathed her, brushed her hair and cut her nails. She no longer played the piano as it hurt her hip to sit on the stool. Her eyesight was growing dim and she preferred to spend her time lying in bed, dreaming and talking to her papa.

On her 74th birthday she woke as the light of the sun crept in under her eyelids. She sighed and smiled and opened her body to let the love into her heart. It was so strong now, so powerful, she never fought it anymore. Each day it became more and more powerful, more seductive, more alluring than having to get up in the cold and wash herself and spend the day by the fire. She had spent several days that week dozing and basking in and out of love. She had forgotten to eat, to drink, to wash herself. She lost herself between the worlds, didn't know now what was real and what was not real. She spent hours talking to her papa, running in fields of green and flowers and meadows while her body still lay in the cold winter room.

This day, she followed the hue of the love, the heavy sweetness of the feeling of it, the strength of the pull of it. She found herself stepping out of herself, looking down at her body for the first time. She suddenly realised how old she had become. No shock though, just noticing. Then she turned and saw her father, still young, still in his 30s as she imagined him to be, every day. This time he was sharper and more in focus, more solid than ever before. He was reaching out for her, his two hands held out to her and a beautiful soft smile on his face. "Come now Françoise, my little limpet, it's time," he said. Her heart lifted, she smiled and reached out to him. Holding hands, they walked together and followed the sunbeams up into the sky.

I Cut Myself

Unthinkingly I lick the wound
tasting my blood then I'm running through the
woods
dark forest leaves and sticks crunch beneath my feet
panting, breathless, I turn and there you are smiling
at me, eyes bright - yes!

This is what we live for
the night air, the moon, the freedom of it all
we run

The rush of air, smells amplified by the night, the
taste of blood
we hear the rabbits hide at our approach but tonight
we hunger for something other
how fast you fly, I fly to keep a pace with you

We are pack, we are pack
I would die for you
in our freedom we are bonded
there is nothing that exists for me other than this
moment

Over ground, miles we travel
we stop to catch our breaths at this lakepond the
reflection of your sheer coat glistens on the water
under moonlit sky
with panting tongues we drink deep
the water splashes up and wets your coat

you shake it out drops flying everywhere and we
dance with joy
we prance together
so happy so free under the blanket of the night and
someone speaks

I turn
and you're nowhere to be found
daylight streams into my eyes
groggy for a moment,

Hard edges, carpet underfoot, this bleeding cut on
my finger I lost myself
somewhere in the in-between
I bring myself back to the here
the pain of tearing myself away contained beneath
my smile

But my heart knows
oh yes my love it knows
we run wild and free in some other place

I'll meet you there

Be With It

My love
Be with your sadness
Allow yourself to feel it
You are safe

Be with your sadness, your guilt, your shame
Your fear of joy
Whatever it is you carry around with you like dead weight
That stops you from your life

Allow yourself to welcome it
Let it in
for it is a part of you
A part of being human
Honour it
The part that finds it so difficult to be here
We all have this part

You are not alone in this
We all have this

And smell the rose anyway
With your sadness
Bring it with you and let it smell the rose too
The rose doesn't care
It's just a rose and wants to be admired
Your sadness just wants to be seen

Spring comes and the grass grows
And we are all made the same way
We are the rose
We are the sadness
And we are one

A Prayer To Let Love In

I take this time to slow down and connect to my breath. I take this time to slow down and remember what love really means. I take the time to separate in my mind manipulation from love.

I ask for help so that I can clear out the mistruths, the emotional pain and the need from my idea of what love is.

I ask to be shown how to change my language in the stories that I am telling about what love means to me.
Love that is needy is not true love.

Love that is desperate is not true love.

I ask the universe to show me what true unconditional love feels like right now.
I am open to it.

I feel safe to accept love into my life now. I soften to love and I let love in and I can feel it immediately. I feel the earth beneath my feet and the sky above me. I bring my presence more and more into this moment.

It is safe to be here; it is safe to let love in.

Help me release my fear of love. Show me how I can bring love more and more into my life. I know that the love I need is already here.

Box

The box you're in also holds the ocean, the sunsets
and beaches. I walk there every day for hours
I am usually in two places at once, I always have
sand in my hair

Unless I'm lying on my bed alone, looking out the
window, then I am here
and my heart turns inside out
and the ocean comes to me

The Work

I can walk without holding on
I can open my eyes and see
I taste
it's my tongue that
tastes and my heart
that longs

I do the work
I undo the work
I piece together the strings and
weave a blanket of silver and gold
that will cover me
when I am dead

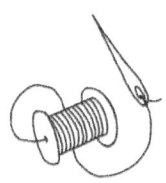

Song Of Woman 2

I am woman
and I love

Endless capacity for love and pain
endless need
for love
and pain

Open heart and body
pockets to be filled
I put the rocks in there myself
the pain reminds me I'm alive

Oh Scarlet Heart if only you were not so demanding

I am woman

Strong
connected
to all things living or once lived
now
past
or unfolding

A conduit
for words already spoken
words as yet unsaid

"I deserve to be happy"

I am woman

And I grieve
for my inner child
I put my arms around her
and love who she was
before she turned into me

I keep my pain
because it's mine

Gaping hole
gaping whole
needs to be filled

Father, brother, son, husband, lover,
man, men, mankind
returning to the strength that bore them
the knowledge that comes through pain
wrapped in our arms
no matter who they are their beginning is the same

Bearer of children
holding a person in our belly
moving distinctly for a while
just visiting

I am woman
I watch as my body expands
it does not belong to me
constant nausea
skin stretched into oblivion

aching back
Forget about this miracle I am making
can't move
can't sleep

No guarantee of
unconditional love
I never had it
how would I recognise it to give it to another?

The pain of birth
Purer than truth

Leftovers
saggy stretched abused carcass
of empty woman
no longer beautiful nor pleine

And we go on
mostly alone
babe chewing at my nipple
crying at midnight, no peace
no space, please
give me grace

I am woman

I see myself in baby's eyes
and my heart softens
essence of mother daughter
nature
Tree branch and blossom

bee that flies between them

Stay now, stay awhile
Rest here in my heart
I will hold you as you fall asleep in my arms
Nurture

You won't be let see those
silver threads connected from
my heart to your wings.

I'll wait for you to leave,
and in the meantime
I'll write an epic poem to be remembered by.

Depression

A dead tree is a dull and lifeless thing.
Whereas a sleeping tree in the throes of winter,
holds potential.
Yes, it is death of a sort
but something in the creeping fibres shows that life's
still present.

I suppose you could liken this to people
dead behind the eyes or dull with
Loss of Soul?

Their Soul has gone to winter to hide in the warm
richness of the mother.
And she will return with the fullness of spring.
Be patient with them
for they will spread their foliage and grand beauty in
their own time.
Let nature take its course.

The Strength Of Cranes

I am fascinated by the strength of cranes
to be lifted by a crane as it stretches its nose into the
cold morning mist
and swings me like concrete from where I am to
where I am going

As I watch tall rigid straightness lifting without
straining
moving without thinking
as small men with shells for hats
dance around it, fussing

My crane is mediumspringgreen
it knows everything
and is not beaten down by the wind

Cat

I would transmogrify into a cat –
jump out the window into the cold night,
leap the tall wall and sit admiring
my own reflection under the moonlight,
momentarily transfixed; until I would
remember my purpose for being here.
Determinedly drop down on four feet
silently, hesitate for a moment,
find my bearings, being now much smaller.
I then would stealth through dark streets to your house
drawn, as a magnet, to its opposite
pole, driven by a force I can't explain
no distraction until I reach my goal
and stop again, outside, to catch my breath.

I hear voices as people say goodnight
rounding up conversation; it is late.
I can pick your voice out and listen close
until they stop. So patiently I wait
to make my entrance hidden from all sight,
creep slowly to the back door, find a crack
and paw it open, pad across the floor,
upstairs to your room. There you are asleep.
I leap beside you, curl about your feet
three times, relaxing, purr myself to sleep.

Prince Sannu

Once upon a time, on a big far away hill, lived Prince Sannu. He had lovely long jet-black hair and blue eyes. He had a horse and a dog and a room full of toys. He had his dinner served on golden plates with golden knives, forks and spoons. He had a small zoo in his garden that had the most beautiful birds and lots of monkeys. He had a view of the land outside his window and his bed was the softest bed in the world.

The prince had everything a little boy could need, but he was not happy. You see, the prince had no brother or sister. The king and the queen were always very busy and did not have time to play with the prince, or even eat with him. They were always meeting important ministers and having very grand dinner parties, no place for a little boy. He was lonely. He wanted someone to play with, but his father the king and his mother the queen had decided long ago that he wasn't allowed to play with the ordinary boys and girls because he was not ordinary. He was the prince.

Sannu would play by himself with his toys for hours making up stories, but he would soon get tired of having to come up with all the storylines himself. He loved to ride on his horse, Darkmaster, in the castle grounds; he would fly over the hedges and bushes, his long hair streaming behind him. But he was not allowed go outside the castle walls. He played with his dog in the long corridors – he'd throw a ball and Paolin would catch it and bring it back to him. But this made him happy only for a while. One time, he took a chimp from his zoo into the castle and brought him in for dinner! That was great fun as the chimp danced on the table and threw food at the servants! It didn't take too long before the chimp climbed up the velvet curtains and started swinging from the chandelier. His father was not happy after that and, to make sure that it never happened again, he sent all the monkeys away to the big zoo in the city. Now, Prince Sannu's zoo had only birds.

Then one day, everything changed. The king summoned Sannu to his room. "Sannu, we have some news," he said. "We are going to have a baby. You will soon have a little brother or sister."

"Oh dear" thought Sannu, "babies mean trouble. If my parents have a baby, they will never have any time for me, and they hardly have any time for me as it is." Sannu was devastated. He had to do something. That night he sat up in bed looking out at the moon and the stars. "I shall run away and see the world for myself," he thought. "Yes, that is what I shall do."

The next day was an ordinary day for Sannu but he had his plan, so when he woke, the day seemed to have a sparkle of magic about it. He was very excited about his secret. He needed to get some things together for his journey and this was the day to collect them. Then that night, he would leave the castle forever. He didn't know what he needed to bring since he had never left the castle before. He did know about money and that if he wanted to buy food to eat, he would probably need some. He didn't have any saved up because, being the prince, he never needed any. But he did know that the spoons were made of gold, and he could probably exchange a spoon for some money. So at breakfast, he managed to slip three spoons into his pocket without anyone seeming to notice.

Sannu realised that everyone would know that he was the prince. He needed a disguise so he decided to wear the clothes of a servant. He had to be clever though if he was to get them. So at noon, Sannu asked if he could have a yoghurt drink made with the berries found in the castle's garden. He knew that it would take the servant boys about an hour to collect enough berries for his royal drink, and then he could sneak into their room and steal some clothes.

At half past noon, Sannu snuck quietly into the quarters and found the room where all the boys slept. He went to the cupboard and opened it and found some clean trousers and a shirt. "Great!" he thought. He looked down at his feet. He wore beautiful slippers with silver thread embroidered into them. He couldn't wear those with these clothes; he would need something plain. But he couldn't find any shoes in amongst the boys clothing, and it was getting late. Sannu was getting anxious, so he left the sleeping quarters quietly and ran back to his room without getting caught.

His heart was beating really fast in his chest and he quickly shoved his new clothes under his bed. He lay panting on his bed staring up at the ceiling until he calmed down. "What more do I need to bring with me?" he wondered. He had spoons for money and now clothes for his disguise. He didn't know what else he needed, so he went out and found Paolin and played with him until dinner.

That night after dinner, he said goodnight as usual to the king and the queen, who hardly even talked to him as they ate because they were so excited about the idea of a new baby. He went up to his room and felt sad about leaving.

"If I do go," thought Sannu, "I won't see Darkmaster or Paolin anymore and I would miss them lots and lots." Sannu flopped down onto his bed. "No, I won't go." He'd stay and be a good prince. And he'd never learn what it is to live. He'd stay, and never learn what it's like to have a friend. No. To learn these things, Sannu thought that he really would have to leave. It was too late to leave then and there. The moon was out and even though it was shining brightly, Sannu didn't want to travel at night. He decided that he would leave the castle just before the sun came up, and he would leave in his disguise.

Sannu removed his princely clothes. He took a silver scissors out of a drawer in his room and stood in front of his mirror in the moonlight. "Here I go," he whispered and he started to cut. His beautiful long hair fell in clumps all around him. It didn't take long before it was cut to the nape of his neck. He brushed himself off and put on the servant boy's clothes. He looked in the mirror again. He didn't even recognise himself. He picked up the clumps of his hairs from the carpet and shoved them into a bag and put the bag inside his wardrobe. Then he sat on his bed to wait.

He must have fallen asleep because the next thing he knew, the sun had already started to rise. "I must leave now," he thought. His hand went to his newly cut hair and he realised that what he was about to do had already begun. He slipped the three spoons into his trouser pocket and made his way barefoot to the servants' quarters so that he could leave the castle by the back gates.

The corridor of the castle was dark. Sannu stopped outside his mother's bedroom door for a moment, and in his heart he knew that she would be very sad without him, but the new baby would be coming soon and she would soon forget. He continued along his way. He saw the door to the servants' quarters and knew that beyond that was the back door, and beyond that again, freedom.

Sannu was breathing fast now and his heart was beating strongly again, just as it did when he was taking the boys clothing. He tried to be quiet as he crept in and saw that the beds were empty. He went past the first bed, and then the second, and then...

"Boy? Where are you going?" shouted a man's voice. Sannu froze. "Are you shirking off your duties? Turn around."

It was Parmeet, the head of the servants. He was tall and dark and the servants were afraid of him. Sannu knew this because he overheard one of the serving boys in the dining room whispering to another one time when they thought nobody was listening. Sannu turned and kept his eyes to the ground, he didn't want to look Parmeet in the face.

"You must mop the floor of the dining hall before the king and queen take breakfast, you know what you have to do – get going NOW!"

Sannu didn't know where the mop and bucket were, and he didn't want to mop the floor. This was not in his plan. He turned away again and his eye caught the back door, only a few feet away. He could run for it.

"BOY NOW!!" shouted Parmeet. Sannu decided to pretend he was going to mop the floor now and, when no one was looking, he could make a run for it later. Sannu faced Parmeet again and nodded his head.

"I'll come with you to make sure you do it," said Parmeet . "You must be new here. I don't recognise you." Parmeet marched Sannu into a small room that had lots of sweeping brushes, mops, buckets, everything you would need if you had to clean a whole castle. "Help yourself to a mop and bucket," said Parmeet, "then come with me and we will fill the bucket with water."

This done, Sannu carried a mop, which was almost twice as long as himself, and a bucket, which was almost twice as heavy, to the dining room.

"Soap! We forgot the soap!" said Parmeet. "I will go get it. You stay here and start mopping."

Sannu was suddenly alone, standing there in his servant's clothes, trapped in his own house. His heart was heavy as his plan had not worked the way he wanted to. But then he realised that he was trapped in the house every day anyway, only he was trapped as a prince! He laughed at this, thinking that at least today something different was happening!

"Laughing now are you? I'm glad you find something funny about this," said Parmeet as he returned and poured the soap into the bucket. "Now mop".

Sannu, had never mopped a floor before so he had no idea how to do it. But Parmeet just stood there watching him so he had no choice but to make his best try. He put the mop into the bucket and sloshed it around a bit, took the mop out and slapped it onto the wooden floor. He started pushing it back and forth and then felt he must be doing it right, except there was a lot of water.

"Have you never mopped a floor before? I must have words with Ananti. She picked you but she didn't know what she was doing. Put some effort into the mop boy. Put your back into it!"

Sannu started mopping faster and harder and felt beads of sweat from the heat and the effort trickling down his face. He saw the floor starting to shine from his work and, suddenly, he realised that he was enjoying himself.

He mopped hard and he mopped long and he mopped the whole dining room floor. All the water in the bucket turned black from the dirt and he didn't realise that Parmeet had left him a long time ago as he was so absorbed by what he was doing. He stood back proud of himself with aching shoulders and pride in his heart.

Sannu remembered his plan and he thought, "I'm alone now, now's my chance," but he still held the mop in his hand. "I'll put the mop away and then I'll leave." He walked back to the cleaning room, mop and bucket in his hand, and put both back into their place yet forgetting to empty the bucket of water.

"BOY! What do you think you are doing with that bucket? Empty it outside at once!"

"That guy doesn't miss a thing," thought Sannu. He turned to go back through the servants' quarters.

"Not that way, through the kitchen." barked Parmeet.

"At least I know where that is," Sannu thought as he turned back and walked towards the kitchen carrying the heavy bucket of dirty water.

In the kitchen there was lots of activity. A royal dinner party was planned for that night, and they were preparing pheasant with apricot and cream sauce. For dessert, there was triple chocolate and cherry tart. The cook was shouting and the servants were running and cutting and they were covered in flour ... there was lots going on. Sannu stopped and stared, he had never actually been inside the kitchen before and seen what went on. He was fascinated. He watched the grinders grind the chocolate beans; he watched the bakers knead the dough for the bread; he watched the girls whipping up the cream, and as he watched, his stomach growled and he realised that he was hungry.

He picked up his bucket and walked through to the other side of the kitchen and out the door. He spilled the dirty water out and went to the apple tree and picked an apple and bit into it. Normally an apple tastes just like an apple but when you've just cut off your own hair and are wearing somebody else's clothes, when you've just spent your first time mopping a floor, and you don't know where you are going next or what is going to happen next, an apple can taste like the most delicious thing you've ever tasted, even if you are a prince. Sannu tasted each bite of that apple, he chewed it slowly and felt the juice trickle down his throat. He decided it was his favourite food, an apple. He smiled. He had never had such an interesting day, nor had he eaten anything as good as this apple.

Suddenly Sannu heard music playing. He forgot he was to leave the castle and followed the sound of the music to find out what it was. Some of the servants had taken out instruments and were playing. Some of the girls danced and their skirts flew around and around as they twisted and moved to the sounds being played from the instruments. The boys were clapping and some started to dance too. They were smiling and laughing and Sannu could not help but be infected by the happiness all around him. His foot was tapping to the music and his legs started moving and, before he knew it, he was whirling around dancing with the others too, whooping with happiness and clapping his hands. He was having the best day. A boy came over to him and smiled.

"Hi. I don't know you; my name is Haroon."

"Hi. I'm....." Sannu didn't know what to say but then thought of his dog. "I'm Paolin."

"Paolin! That's the name of the princes dog. That's really funny!" Haroon laughed.

Sannu smiled. "I didn't know that." he said.

"Will you help me with Darkmaster?" asked Haroon. "I have to clean his stable."

Sannu thought it would be great to see his horse one more time before he left. He then realised that he never thought about where his horse lived. He never thought about what went on in the kitchens, who cleaned the floors, or who made his bed. He never had to think about any of these things, being the prince. He was beginning to realise how little he knew about anything in the castle.

Sannu said, "I would love to help you in the stable. Will you tell me what to do?"

The two boys walked away from the gardens and the music faded into the distance. They walked past the fountain that was in the shape of a star and past the statue of the king on a horse and past the statue of Sannu's grandfather, also on a horse.

"How long have you been working in the castle? asked Haroon. I don't remember seeing you here."

"I'm just new," said Sannu. "I only got here today."

"Ahh," said Haroon. "That explains why you look so lost! We're nearly at the stables now."

The stables were in a stone building that had a thatched roof, and Sannu was not surprised when he realised he had never noticed this building before.

"Everything is new today," he thought. When they walked inside, the smell hit him, a heavy and pungent aroma of horse manure. New straw was piled up in bales at the side of the stable.

"We have to sweep out all the old straw and the muck. When that's done, we have to lay down new straw for the horse's bed," said Haroon. "Ok, here take this." Haroon handed Sannu a pitchfork. "Be very careful not to stick it in your foot by mistake!"

Sannu looked down at his feet and saw how dirty they were from his day working in the castle. He looked at Haroon's feet and saw that not only were they dirty, but they looked like the feet of an older man, rough from long years of walking barefoot. His feet looked baby soft and new, compared to Haroon.

Sannu thought he would look in to see Darkmaster before he started to work. "Where are the horses?" asked Sannu.

"They run in the field during the day," said Haroon. "The best time to clean out the stable is when they are not here."

Sannu was disappointed. Haroon started working, dragging out the dirty straw with his pitchfork. Once he managed to get a pile together, he would stick the fork into it and lift it up into the air and then throw it into a large wooden box, which was on wheels. Sannu started doing it too. He found the pitchfork to be very heavy yet, after a while, he managed to make a pile of dirty straw too, but it really wasn't as easy as Haroon made it look.

"You have enough straw there now Paolin," said Haroon. "Try to put it into the box."

Sannu tried to balance some dirty straw on the end of his pitchfork and lift it up, but it kept falling off!

"You have to really dig the fork in, like this." Haroon did it and made it look really easy. After a few times, Sannu got a small bit of straw into the box. He smiled to himself. Even though it was so hot and smelly in the stable, he was happy to work beside Haroon.

"Darkmaster won't know it was me that made her bed tonight!" he thought, and he smiled, remembering all the joy that Darkmaster had given to him. Mucky, dirty and smelling like straw from a horse's bed, Sannu and Haroon finished laying the fresh straw for the horse and walked back to the castle. The afternoon light was turning deep yellows and oranges, and Sannu knew that it would be nearly time for dinner. He wondered if his mother missed him at all today or if his father noticed he was gone.

"Ananti will have food ready for us," said Haroon. "Let's go wash first. We're both very dirty after all that hard work." Sannu smiled and followed Haroon into the servants' quarters. Haroon went into a small room off to the side from where the beds are and Sannu followed. There he found five large tubs of water. Haroon took off his clothing and stepped into one of the tubs of water and washed himself. Sannu did the same. The coolness of the water felt good against his hot skin, and he sank into the tub and closed his eyes.

"You are tired," laughed Haroon. "Come don't fall asleep now. The best part of the day is about to begin!"

"How could things get any better than they are already?" thought Sannu.

Haroon got out and dried himself, picked up his dirty clothes and ran naked into the sleeping area. Sannu got out of the tub too and did the same, wondering what was going to be next for the day. All thoughts of leaving the castle had vanished from his mind. As he picked up his clothes, he felt the spoons in the pocket of the trousers. His heart missed a beat. He took the clothes and dropped them into the pile with the rest of the dirty clothes. He realised he couldn't take the spoons out of the trousers, so he put the dirty trousers back on again.

"Don't wear those. They need to be washed," said Haroon.

"But I don't have another pair," said Sannu.

"Here take these." Haroon handed him a pair of trousers from the cupboard. Sannu had no choice but to take off his dirty trousers, leave the spoons in the pocket and put on the clean pants. He didn't know what he was going to do.

"Come on, I can smell the food." Haroon took Sannu's hand and ran to the kitchen. Sannu was so tired now, his eyes were closing and he wondered how Haroon had so much energy. They went to a long room behind the kitchen, one Sannu had never been in before. There was a long low table full of plain white plates piled high with delicious smelling food, all different types of beautiful things to eat. Around the table sat the girls and boys who danced earlier in the day. They were chatting and eating using their fingers, feeding each other, laughing, joking and smiling. Everyone was happy. Sannu felt new energy rush into his body as he was brought to the table and introduced to everyone.

"This is Paolin," said Haroon. "He started today."

"I didn't know anyone new was starting today," said one of the girls and they welcomed him. "Here, take this." One girl handed him an empty plate.

Haroon whispered, "That's Daharini. She is the second head of the girls." Haroon stretched across into the table and grabbed some food and put it on his plate. Sannu copied him and lifted some up from the plate then and into his mouth. It was delicious. Not as grand a dish as he was used to having; it almost looked like leftovers on the plate, but the flavours were really strong on his tongue.

"Just like the apple," he thought, "everything tastes better today!"

They talked and laughed with everyone in the room. Then after dinner, the servants scattered to different chores, and Sannu and Haroon were left to tidy up all the plates and bring them back to the kitchen. Sannu wondered as he was tidying up what he would do next. He could return to his room, sneak back there and be the prince again. Or he could sleep in the servants quarters and try and run away again tomorrow. Just as he was trying to figure it all out, there was a gong banging and shouting outside.

Haroon said, "Something must be wrong." The boys put the plates down on the table and looked out the door to see what was going on.

"All male servants report to the sleeping quarters at once." It was Parmeet.

"Uh oh," thought Sannu, "this cannot be good.

He was right to be worried. Parmeet was standing in the sleeping quarters holding three golden spoons in his hand.

"Who dares to steal from our king?" his loud voice bellowed out and all the servants cringed. "Never before has anyone dared to steal. The penalty is too high. Own up and face your consequences."

Sannu didn't know what to do so he stayed still. "I know who you are," said Parmeet. "You have one chance to own up or I will arrest you myself. Either way you will be punished." Nobody moved.

Sannu thought, "Ok, he knows it's me. I should own up. I can tell him who I am and everything will be alright ."

"I know it's you because I found the spoons in your trouser pocket. What did you think you were going to do with them? Haroon, come to me NOW."

Haroon froze and then looked at Sannu with panic in his eyes. Parmeet grabbed Haroon by the back of the neck before he could move and lifted him up by his shirt. The look of shock on Haroon's face really upset Sannu and he knew he had to do something.

In a quiet voice, Sannu said, "No it wasn't him; it was me."

"Who said that?" shouted Parmeet.

A voice from inside Sannu spoke to him: "Remember you are a prince; now you need to act like a prince." Sannu stood up to his full height and said strongly, "They are my spoons. They are not stolen. I am the prince. I am Sannu."

Quiet hushed through the room. Nobody believed it.

"Sannu?" whispered Haroon, "but you told me your name was Paolin," and as he said it, he knew where the name came from.

Sannu stood proud in his bare feet and his servants clothing and said, "I am Prince Sannu and I demand that you let Haroon go. Anything you have to say, you can say to me."

Parmeet looked at Sannu for a long, long time. Even though the boy had short hair and did not look like the prince, he stood tall like a prince. Parmeet saw the strength and courage in the boy's eyes and was wise enough to know that even though he may be wearing servants clothing and have the short hair of a common boy, these were only on the outside. He put Haroon down on the floor and motioned to everyone in the room to go. They left quickly and quietly. It was just Parmeet and Sannu then.

"What are you doing here your majesty?" asked Parmeet, and then he remembered the morning duties, the floor mopping. "You are the boy who didn't know how to mop a floor?" A sparkle came into his eye and he started to laugh. Sannu relaxed a little. He knew that everything was going to be ok.

"Yes. I mopped the floor and I enjoyed mopping the floor. For lunch, I ate an apple that I picked myself from a tree. I danced in the garden with the servants, and I helped Haroon clean the stable. I just ate the best dinner of my life, and I just had the best day of my life." Parmeet understood.

"What do you wish to do with me?" asked Sannu.

"That depends," said Parmeet.

"Depends on what?" said Sannu, worried that Parmeet was going to talk to his father about everything that he did today.

"It depends on what YOU want," said Parmeet. "You think about what it is you want. Go now to your room and think about it. Then come and find me tomorrow and we can talk. I can see from your actions that you are a man of honour. I shall honour you by not telling your father directly. But if you do not come to me in the morning, this will change."

"Thank you," said Sannu, and he left the servants' quarters.

Sannu walked back to his own room, went inside and closed the door behind him. He felt very different to the boy who left his room only a few hours ago. He took off the servant's clothes, brushed his teeth, washed his face and looked at himself in the mirror. He looked like Sannu all right; he was still himself. He put on his princely pyjamas and slipped between the silky sheets of his bed. Before he even had time to think about what he was supposed to think about, he fell asleep.

Sannu fell into a deep dream. He dreamt that he was in a big field not knowing where he was, feeling lost and alone. He climbed a hill and looked out over many fields. Not very far away he saw flames and smoke, and when he looked closer, he couldn't believe what he saw - a dragon! Men were fighting the dragon and the dragon was blasting fire out at them. It was terrible. The people were screaming and yelling for help. Sannu noticed that the people were attacking only the front of the dragon. The back of the dragon was exposed, but if people were to fight the dragon from behind, they might have a chance. He decided he had to go tell the men and help them. He ran down the hill and started shouting but nobody heard him. He tried to shout louder but his voice was lost in amongst the screaming and the fear. Sannu decided he would do this job himself, so he picked up a spear from the ground and got in close to the smoke and the flame and tried to help. The dragon turned to him and looked him in the eye. It was the scariest thing he had ever seen. The dragon started to move towards him and, covered in sweat and breathing fast, Sannu woke up and it was morning. He knew what he had to do.

He put on his princely clothes. He brushed his short chopped hair. He was as ready as he ever would be. He went down the long hallway and found Parmeet.

"I am the prince," said Sannu to Parmeet, "and when I grow up, I will be king. But I don't know very much about the world. Sometimes I get very lonely. But I know I will be a good king. I will stay here in the castle and take my lessons. I will ride my horse and play with my dog and study my books. But sometimes, I will dress as a serving boy and come among you and spend the day as a servant. I want to be treated exactly the same way as all the other servants. This way I will also be learning, learning about real life. This will make me a better king when it is my time."

Parmeet put his hand on Sannu's shoulder. "I am proud of you, young prince. Very proud. You are welcome here at any time, on any day. I will never speak to you like this again while you wear your princely clothes. But if you come to me in servant's clothing, you will be treated as a servant, and maybe then if you want to, we can talk some more."

Sannu nodded. Then he walked away. As he walked, he felt that he did indeed discover a new land, a new land inside his old one. And as he went into the dining room to eat breakfast with his parents, he noticed for the first time, how clean the floor looked.

Growth Hurts

The egg must crack and smash to let the creature
within spread its wings.

We are the egg
but we also are the wings that fly
born onto a moving platform where nothing stays
the same
Although our brain would like to tell us otherwise.

People grab fistfuls of each other
tearing each other apart trying to catch a hold of
something to anchor into
while the earth is spinning below.

Defy logic and
cast your hook deep into that which spins
and spin with it
and crack and break and hatch and grow and fly,

Fly my pretty
for you forgot you have wings
and the sky awaits.

A Prayer For Healing

Dear God,

Please connect me to a source of pure healing
energy and let it into my heart

I open to allow it flow through my body
I surrender all of my fear to it
I allow it wash away my doubt and I ask it to give me
the strength that I need to continue to shine my light
to the world

May there be Grace in every breath,
May there be Grace in every step that I take today.

Help me walk the path of light
With you at my side
I can be a guiding light for those who are still in the
darkness

Amen

Pink Ribbons

A desert
A single tree
branches bare blue sky and clouds

Like Arizona
dry air
me only and this tree
I have been here before

I walk towards the tree slowly and see
that in its branches are wisps of pink ribbon
translucent and moving
weaving back and forth as if in a breeze as if behind
the tree there is a fan
but there is no wind only this heat and the
brightness of the sky

I look at the tree more closely
looking for my heart
but I retrieved that already
I took it back the first time I came here
Hands move to chest and touch and remember how
it felt
I am at the centre once again

But still
these pink wisps shreds
are they the ribbons of my Soul?

I recognise them now
and it explains why I've been going around in circles
feeling like I haven't filled my body
Floating between worlds
feeling vulnerable and small and this
constant crying

I call to the pink ribbons dancing in the windless sky
"Come back to me, Oh how I've missed you"
And then
they turn into small swallows and leave the tree
fly towards me as a rush
I get a sense of joy
as I stand there and watch them revel in their
freedom

Feel the hot air moving underneath their wings my
wings as
quickly they surround me and fly past me and
through me and then they are gone

I turn to the tree, the pink ribbons are also gone
and suddenly I am whole again
connected

I can feel the difference distinctly
I look at my feet, my hands
move about as if I'm wearing a new dress which
clings to me
Sweeps this way that way and look how it trails
behind me glistening

Yes!
It's all here
my Soul is all here!
And I am here!

The tree
now standing empty
bows its bough
and I bow back
knowing I can come here any time I need
and do it all again

We Are Getting Stronger

We don't realise that we are actually getting stronger.

It's about riding the waves of it, not being smashed by them into fragments and pieces of shattered glistening particles of light.

We forget that within us lies the answers to all things
Perhaps poetry will forge the path through the darkness
or perhaps we can simply light a torch and
shine it outwards
to see where we are going to.

Has it evolved yet?
Does it exist yet?
Do we make it?

Never before have we come this far, and yet there is a holding pattern, comfort in the geometry that holds it, all of it, together.

They are all waking up now.

Choices need making.
Bedclothes need folding.
The bread is warm in the oven.

Master Of Time

Long fleshy tendrils hanging like gypsy beads over a doorway my head tangled in thick candyfloss clouds weaving patterns between the betweens to find the most favourable outcome

Then part the waves to go, there and there, again release releasing into it shifting the universe, bend it shape it in synchrony with the breath believing its true calling the Angels by name I hear them singing to me as I sleep and untangle myself from the dark

Enlightenment

I'm glad I didn't kill myself those few times in my life when I really wanted it all to end.
For now I see that we have to die to ourselves and pass through the gate of our limitations
Before the expanse of the onwards opens up to us
So we can move through it and up to the next learning, the next lesson, the next level
To do it all again.

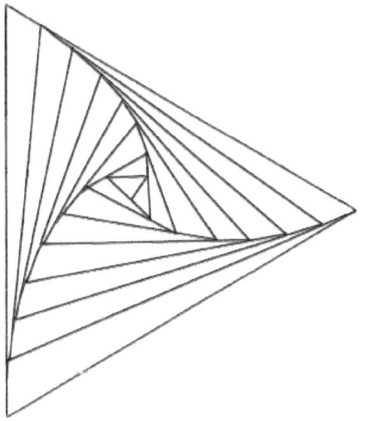

The Magical Boy

Once upon a time, there was a little boy who loved nature. His name was Andrew. When he was three years old he wandered off from his family's picnic, part-way into the forest beside where they were sitting, and found an interesting spot right beside a fairy tree. He hunkered down, as three-year-olds do, so he could explore. He lifted rocks and laughed to see the earwigs crawling out from under them. He touched leaves and felt the textures between his fingers. He picked up and licked different coloured stones to understand what they were made of. And right at the base of the root of the tree, he turned over the grassy mounds and saw a glittering thing.

He was very much attracted to glittering things, so he picked it up and held it to the sky. It was so small, it pressed into his fingers as the sunlight shone through it, and it was red and beautiful and looked like a diamond, as if he had ever seen a diamond before, but he hadn't. He rolled it around between his thumb and index finger, and then he heard a noise – was it a fox? He stood up, moss falling off his legs as he rose, and turned around to face the direction of the noise. As he did so, he popped the red glittery thing into his mouth and swallowed it without even realising he was doing it. He heard the noise again; it was his mother calling his name, so he wandered out of the forest and back into her arms.

Over the next 15 years, the glittery thing grew inside him. It stuck in his throat for a while. He tried to cough it up for a week and his mother kept giving him cough mixture. Then after a while, it moved down deeper into his throat and into his chest. It travelled around inside him for a year or so until it found a home just above his heart. As it settled inside him, it grew and, once it reached a certain size, it sent out feathery cords, just as nerve cells do. These feathery cords attached themselves to his nerves, and the red glittery thing became like a spiderweb inside him. But it hung there and did nothing, and Andrew felt nothing and went on with his life.

One day when he was 24 Grace went to Egypt to visit the pyramids. Grace really liked Andrew, but Andrew was not sure if he liked Grace, so they had gone on a few dates. Grace was hoping for more. She was thinking about him when she entered the Kings' Chamber in the Grand Pyramid of Egypt, and when her tour guide called on the Angels and the Ancient Kings and Queens of Egypt to come and sing for them and with them and to them, the chamber activated and the strongest of the strong Egyptian energies flooded into the chamber and the whole chamber was alight with its power. Of course, to the human eye nothing could be seen, but everybody who was in that chamber on that day could feel it, and they said that something in their lives changed because of it. That power lit up everyone in the chamber, it flowed through all of them, they had power coursing through their veins, including Grace, who lit up from her head to her toes. She was still thinking about Andrew as the energy poured through her and out from her, and some of this energy leapt from her heart and travelled across space and time faster than the speed of light and went straight into Andrew's heart.

Andrew was playing a football match at the exact moment that Grace was in the King's Chamber. When the energy went from her and into him, he suddenly found himself quite winded and he fell down abruptly onto his backside. He didn't know what had hit him, he thought it was the ball, but when he looked down at his arms there was no ball at all. Puzzled, he looked up to see where the ball was and saw that all of the players were running about at the other end of the pitch. Andrew was alone on the ground, mucky, winded and confused, and nobody even seemed to have noticed. He wondered what had happened, and he shook and scratched his head and saw the players coming back up the field towards him, so he got up quickly and ran over to the other players and went back into the game. Later that night, he was singing with his team in the pub celebrating their 3-1 win and had totally forgotten about what had happened. But somewhere deep inside Andrew's chest a not so little red glittery thing had started pulsating. The pulses flowed through the flowery tendrils that held that red glittery thing in place. And Andrew, of course, had no idea that this was happening.

Over the next few weeks the glittery red thing started glowing and growing and the pulsations became stronger. These pulsations of energy were also red and they leapt out of Andrew's body from time, but he didn't see them or feel them as human eyes were not made to see things at that spectrum of vibration and frequency. But fairy eyes were, and a fairy just happened to be passing by not too long after the incident at the football game. When this fairy saw the red lights around Andrew, she thought they were beautiful, mesmerizingly beautiful, hypnotizingly beautiful. She followed Andrew around that day for several hours. She didn't even realise she was doing it. Then something caught her attention and, when she stopped being entranced by the red lights, she noticed it had gotten dark. She became worried as she knew she had to go home. Once she was at home, she realised that she had not been feeling well all day, so she made herself a cup of elderflower tea, and immediately felt better. Then she remembered the red lights, and not feeling so good, and time seeming to pass so quickly for her. She thought it was very strange that she had forgotten about it, for fairy minds never forget anything. But she had never seen anything like it before and wanted to find out if anyone else had, so she put on her shawl and flew to visit her best friend and told her all about it.

    The news spread that very night from two fairies to four, and then more. All the fairy friends were gossiping about a boy-man with red energy that was beautiful. They were fascinated and wanted to see it too, but it meant sneaking away from their duties. Fairies are mischievous and love a good adventure, so early the next day six excited fairies managed to convince the first fairy that it was a really good idea to go find this boy-man. They all snuck out of their village and went back to the place where the fairy had seen Andrew. But the boy-man was not at the football field and he was not in the pub. They didn't know where he went. Fairies are very determined creatures, so they resolved to split up and search for him. They went all around the town in twos and a three. At lunchtime, the first group of two found Andrew in the park sitting under a tree eating a chicken sandwich and a bag of salt and vinegar crisps. The fairies who found him saw the red lights and became instantly entranced and flew about his shoulders and his face, mesmerised by their glittery pulsations. Fairies love nature, especially trees, so it wasn't long before the other fairies found them. They saw the lights too and also became entranced. Seven fairies hovered around Andrew's face, neck and chest for as long as they could, keeping a little distance away so he would not notice them. When the night fell and before the moon came up, they noticed it was dark and raced back home to the fairy village.

Afterwards, all the fairies could think about was being around the light of the red glittery thing. They dreamt about it. Whenever they saw something red, they got excited and couldn't help themselves. They had to find it and be near it. So every day, instead of doing their chores, seven fairies snuck out of the fairy village and flew to find Andrew. They were getting to know his habits, where he lived, where he worked, what he liked to do in between. They learned his name, but they weren't at all interested in him really; they just followed him around as they watched the little red lights sparking and pulsing and hypnotising them. Andrew had become a magnet for fairies and didn't know anything about it until one day while walking down the usual street to his usual place, surrounded by the usual fairies, he got a text message from Grace asking him to please reconsider their relationship. She told him that he was amazing and that she really wanted to be his girlfriend. He didn't want a relationship with Grace, and he got quite upset with her begging him in a text message. He panicked a little, wondering what he was going to say in reply, and as he was still walking and not really paying attention to where he was going while re-reading her message for the third time, he walked straight into a lamppost and banged his head and ended up sitting on the ground on his backside again, this time on the street.

The fairies got a shock too. They didn't expect this to happen and they saw he was hurt once they pulled themselves away from the glittering of the lights. One of the fairies actually had a little crush on Andrew. She liked the way the light played with his hair and his brown soft kind eyes. She had pointed this out to the others back at her house one night over a pot of tea, so the others took a look at him the following day and found him quite beautiful too. (Fairies are very attracted to beauty as you might have already figured out.) The little fairy who was quite fond of Andrew rushed over to him and stroked his head to make him feel better, and then she recoiled in shock at her boldness. Andrew groaned with pleasure and pain and the fairy got such a fright that she flew right back to the village and straight into her house. She spent all night fretting, playing the sound of his groan over and over in her mind, wondering if he had felt her stroking his head since most humans couldn't feel fairies when they touched them. She started to drive herself crazy thinking that maybe Andrew would notice her, and she wanted to see him and try it again even more than she wanted to see the glittering lights.

The next day the fairy woke up and was feeling quite bold and mischievous with the early morning sun and all the better for having had a good night's sleep so she left earlier than usual, without her friends, to go and find Andrew. He was already in his workplace, sitting at a desk looking at a big screen. The red sparkles were quieter than usual but still quite mesmerising, and for a moment she forgot what she wanted to do. And then she remembered. This fairy crept right up to him and hovered by his ear. There were no other fairies around him; it was just herself and Andrew. She could hear his breathing and the noise of his fingers on the keyboard as he was typing, and she felt the heat from his body and she felt a little bit faint. She touched his ear and he turned around towards her quickly, then brushed her away as if she was a fly. Fairies move quickly so she was not hurt, and with racing heart, she determined to try it again. She took a deep breath and went back to his ear, hovering there, enjoying the closeness of him, becoming intoxicated by the smell of his aftershave. She held out her hand and rubbed his ear. He jumped and turned around and she flew out the door of the room he was in and hid behind a potted plant.

 The rest of the fairies arrived at their usual time, about 20 minutes later, and saw their friend amongst the leaves of the plant and wondered what was going on. She was still a little shaken, and they confronted her until she admitted what had happened. They laughed at her but thought that this would be great fun and wanted to try it too, so all seven fairies went back into the room where Andrew was and spent a few moments admiring the beautiful red glittery thing in his chest which had grown even bigger from all of their attention. It seemed like it was calling to them, saying "Come closer, come closer, let me see you".

They shook their heads to snap out of that feeling, for a red glittery thing in a human's chest talking to them was just nonsense, wasn't it? One of the fairies flew up to the top of Andrew's head and felt much happier there because that glittery red thing wasn't in her line of vision, obscuring her thoughts. She looked at his thick black hair. She wanted to roll around in it and grab handfuls of it, so she stroked his head tentatively and the sound of typing stopped for a moment and then resumed. She rubbed Andrew's head again, feeling a little braver. It was stronger this time, and he jumped and stood up from the desk and turned around, frightening all of the fairies who were watching what was happening. They all quickly flew out of the room and went back to their fairy village so they would not get caught.

The light in Andrew's chest got even stronger. It became more visible, so soon even more fairies saw it so seven became eight, then twelve, then twenty-two. One day hardly any fairies at all showed up in the village to do their daily tasks. The mayor of the fairy village was deeply frustrated and angry. Having been kept in the dark, he resolved to find out what was going on. He called a meeting of all the fairy folk at the village square and demanded to know what was happening and where they all were going.

The meeting happened at night, so all the fairies where back in the village, and one of the newer fairies told the mayor about the red glittery thing and the man who had it in his chest and that they had to see this red glittery thing because it was speaking to them and telling them things.

In the meantime, Andrew was having a very difficult time. He didn't know what was happening to him. He kept being touched and prodded, and he would turn around and there was nobody there. He was having very strange dreams. He heard things being whispered into his ear, he thought he was imagining laughter that sounded like the tinkling of lots of little bells and he wasn't sleeping well. One time it seemed like he had been punched in the stomach. He thought he was going crazy. He didn't want to tell any of his friends because he imagined that they would think he was crazy too.

Andrew worked as a computer programmer in a large international office, and every once in a while the company would take its employees on a day out. Each time it was different. Once they went to the Guinness storehouse and saw how Guinness was made. This time they went to the races, and everyone got €50 to spend on betting, "Just for fun". Andrew never placed a bet before in his life, and he had never been to the races, so he wasn't too keen to go on the day out. However, management didn't appreciate not being appreciated, so he went along regardless. Little did he know that he had brought

18 fairies with him too. Fairies love horses (of course) and they know horses, and they had grown to like Andrew even though they continued to torment him. As Andrew looked at the list of names of the horses running in the first race, one of the fairies whispered in his ear, "Agamemnon". Andrew at this stage expected noise and interference and it was getting him down, making him sad, and he was always trying to ignore it. As his eyes scanned down the list of horses names running in the first race, he did indeed see one of the horses was named Agamemnon. This was very strange. He really wasn't bothered about the whole thing, so he thought to himself, "What the heck," and he placed the whole €50 on Agamemnon to win.

"Do you know something we don't?", asked one of his friends who was afraid to spend more than €2 on the race. "I thought you never did this before?"

"Ahh, I just have a good feeling about this horse," said Andrew shrugging his shoulders and handing over the money.

They went to the stands to watch the race, and once it began, everyone was shouting for all of the horses. Agamemnon was in the last few, but Andrew wasn't really worried either way. He thought at least he would have spent the money and he might sneak out and go home for the rest of the day. Then, Agamemnon picked up speed and began passing out the other horses, slowly at first. As he passed one it was as if he became more interested in running, and he passed another, got faster again and then passed another, until soon he was up in the top three. Andrew found himself screaming with the crowd: "Agamemnon!! GO! GO! GO!", with adrenalin pumping through his veins. He was jumping up and down as the horse now moved into second in the race, and with hardly any time left right at the finish line, Agamemnon pulled his neck out and crossed the finish line first.

"WOW!!", said Andrew's friends to Andrew! "Lucky break you! You won €300!"

"€300? really?"

"Oh yes!!" For the first time, Andrew felt like something was finally going his way.

The fairies were jumping for joy. They were so happy they were able to do something nice for Andrew, and as he received the money in his hand, the red glittery thing shone brighter, and the fairies became energised from it and wanted to do more nice things for Andrew because it felt so good to be around him when he was happy.

Andrew left the races with €2000 in his pocket and a big smile on his face, and that was after he had bought everybody drinks when the tab from his office had run out. He was singing as he walked, taking the long way back through the park when he stopped by his favourite tree, the one he would sit under to eat his lunch.

"Hello tree," he said to the tree. "I don't know what has happened to me but today I knew all the names of the winning horses and I have lots of money in my pocket and all the guys at work got excited and I'm happy, so very happy!"

Andrew didn't know that beside him there was a homeless man who heard him say "I've got lots of money in my pocket." Unfortunately for Andrew, this man was a drug addict and desperately wanted another hit, so he came out from the bush and hit Andrew in the face, took his money and left him there, under the tree, and went to find his dealer with a hop and a skip in his step.

When you deal with fairies, there is always a price.

The few fairies who were brave enough to be out after dark with Andrew were shocked, of course. They had seen humans treating other humans this way before but never their Andrew. They had become quite possessive of him, and they tried to wake him up. They could see the swelling of his eye and the bruising coming up on his cheek, and he had a split lip as well. Trickles of blood dripped across his face and down his neck onto his shirt. What should they do? What should they do?

They looked around and saw a flower and asked permission to take some of its pollen. The flower said yes, and so they brought the pollen to Andrew and stuffed it into his nose, and he sneezed and woke up. Rubbing his face, he noticed that his eye really hurt, and when he looked at his hand, it was covered in blood. His watch was gone, and the money in his pocket was also gone, but he still had his wallet and the keys to his flat so not all was lost.

The next day his friends were slapping him on the back but then saw his face and the bruise and his split lip, and they knew what happened. The first aider in the building said he wouldn't need stitches and gave him some paracetamol, and he sat in front of his computer but couldn't focus on his work at all. This really made no sense. No sense AT ALL. He was tense and fragile and waiting to be poked and prodded again, but after the incident in the park the fairies pulled back a little bit to give Andrew, and themselves, some space.

It didn't last for very long. The draw of the red glittery thing was too strong, and soon they were back plaguing poor Andrew with their whispers and hair pulling and tapping on his shoulder. Now that they knew he could hear them, they would often times tell him what to do, things like what to eat and what to buy, where to go and what to say when he wrote a text message. Because he was so worn down from their attentions, he would more often than not follow their instructions just as a robot would do for its master. Sometimes what he did worked out in his favour, but sometimes it worked against him, and he would end up being hurt or upset or have an argument with a stranger. Life was becoming very bitter for Andrew. He was coming closer to sinking into a great depression. But the fairies were having a great time and didn't seem to notice.

Meanwhile back in the fairy village, the mayor had declared that anyone missing their daily chores would be in big trouble, but nobody paid him any attention whatsoever. He was angry with everyone and everyone in the village simply ignored him.

Andrew started calling in sick to work. He would hide under his duvet repeating "Go away go away" as hordes of fairies hovered around him, pulling at his bedclothes. The glittery red thing was stronger than ever, drawing them to him, and their presence was oppressive. Of course, to the human eye Andrew just looked pale and grey and a little bit crazy, especially when he was batting his arms around himself and muttering, "Leave me alone".

Grace was really worried about him. She knew someone who knew someone who said they knew a shaman healer and she thought perhaps Andrew should go see her. She didn't care anymore that Andrew didn't want her to be his girlfriend. She only cared that Andrew wasn't well, really obviously wasn't well, and she wanted to help him get better. She called around to his flat one day and found him crying under the duvet, so she texted her friend, got the number of the healer and made an appointment for him. He agreed to go. He was ready to try anything.

Andrew managed to get to the healer's office on time. He was unshaven and his face was gaunt and grey. He had lost weight and had developed a nervous twitch from where the fairies were touching and rubbing and pulling at him. He really wasn't feeling like himself anymore: he had lost his sparkle, his zest for life. He didn't care about anything anymore. He was going to the healer only because Grace had told him to, and at this stage he was used to following instructions. He didn't expect this healer would change anything. He was beginning to think about killing himself. He couldn't stand living this way for much longer. Only the week before, he almost walked out in front of a car. He felt like he had been pushed into it and pulled back again just in time. His body was not his own, and he didn't care about anything.

    The healer was a woman in her 50s with long silvery grey hair. She felt soft and warm and familiar to Andrew. Her room smelt of sage and lemons and something else sweet that he didn't know the name of. She ushered him to an armchair and invited him to sit into it. She took a long look at him, up and down, and walked around his chair burning sage and rattling her rattle. He didn't have the energy to feel upset or nervous by her behaviour, and once the rattling stopped, Andrew realised he was thirsty, but he didn't have the energy to ask for a drink of water. The healer poured him a large glass of water and handed it to him. He drank it all down in one go. She refilled his glass and then sat in the chair opposite him. The water was cool and refreshing, and he started to relax a little bit.

"How long has this been going on?" she asked, and he told her he didn't know but it seemed like forever.

"One year? Two years?" Andrew shrugged his shoulders.

"Hmm. Do you remember a time when you felt really happy?" Besides from the brief time that he won the money he thought back in his mind and he remembered the singing in the pub after the football match.

"I was playing football and we won 3-1," he said. "I like football."

"Let me tune into you," said the healer. "I need to consult with my Spirit guides." The healer closed her eyes and went into her heart and visited a place that was far away but also right here. She walked up a tall rocky mountain and stood at the top of it catching her breath. She could see all the landscape below. At the foot of the mountain was a glassy lake, the reflection shone up at her like a looking glass.

"Show me," she said to the lake, and an image formed, fuzzy at first, of Andrew at three years old in the summertime, in the forest, running around and laughing, hunkering down by a tree and picking something up, looking at it, then putting it into his mouth. It was the red thing.

"Hmm this has been going on for a very long time," she said to herself. "What do I need to know to help this man?"

The lake clouded over and another image slowly formed, of Andrew walking to work, with a strong red glittery thing pulsating in his chest and hordes of fairies following him, mesmerised by the glowing lights.

"Ahh," the healer said. "Show me how to remove the red thing from this man's chest please." The lake clouded over, and the healer felt a strong feminine presence appear beside her. She turned and there was the Goddess Erú, for whom Ireland was named. The healer bowed deeply and Erú bowed to the healer.

"Great Goddess, it is wonderful to see you here; I am honoured with your presence."

The Goddess smiled and said, "I have come to claim what is mine, and in doing so, I will put to rights what has been done wrong".

The healer nodded. She looked much older than her 50 years. She looked more like 500 years. Her hair had grown longer, and she had plaits with ribbons and colourful feathers woven in. Goddess Erú was tall and bright and colourful in a crushed green velvet dress, and her beautiful red hair was gently blowing all around her even though there was no wind.

"And what reparations will be made for the human?"

The Goddess replied, "Order will be restored, and he will find himself again."

"Compensation?" asked the healer.

"We shall see," said the Goddess.

"Good," said the healer, and both women nodded towards each other; the deal had been done. Then a great powerful love poured from Erú outwards to fill the landscape, and the Healer could not help but blossom in its presence.

"Come then," the healer said to the Goddess, and they both stepped off the mountain and into the healing room where Andrew had drifted into a slumber.

The Goddess Erú looked at Andrew and breathed on him, and the red glittery thing became visible to human eyes.

"How do we get it out?" asked the healer.

"That is your job, not mine," said the Goddess. So the healer closed her eyes and said her healing prayer and asked her healing guides to come and help her. They came and they helped her, but it was complicated because the glittery red thing thought that it was part of Andrew's body, and Andrew's body thought the glittery red thing belonged to it.

The Goddess Erú banished all the fairies from the room as the healer and her guides worked, and with their absence and her presence the colour began to come back into Andrew's face, yet he stayed sleeping.

"Replacement," whispered the healing guides to the healer.

"So replace it," said the healer to the guides, and they left and came back with a blue shiny thing that was cool and white and soft to the touch, but not the same shape as the glittery red thing. They sat in a circle and looked at the blue shiny thing, and it started to change its shape.

When they had looked at it for long enough and the shape was close enough, the healer said, "Now," and the healing guides put an energetic hospital tent around Andrew's body and gave him a strong anaesthetic. They opened up his aura and cut out the glittery red thing from his body and replaced it with the cool, blue white thing. There was a shaky moment when they didn't know what would happen next, but then Andrew's body seemed to accept the blue thing in replacement, so they handed the red thing to Erú. It was no longer glittery and had a crack right down the middle of it, and then they proceeded to complete their operation.

The healer studied Erú who was looking at the not so shiny glittery red cracked thing in her hand as the healing guides finished their work. They closed Andrew up and removed the hospital tent from around his body. He was snoring lightly, totally oblivious to what had been going on. They gave him an antidote to the anaesthetic and Andrew slept on.

Erú concentrated hard and tightened her grip around the broken red thing and then crushed it. When she opened her hand, it had turned to dust. With the healer watching her every move, she closed her hand again and blew on it gently, and when she opened it a second time, the dust had turned into a perfectly proportioned shiny red ruby. From her pocket Erú pulled out a tiny golden crown that had a space in the front of it for such a ruby. She popped the ruby into the crown, and there was a sound like the sound your tongue makes off of the roof of your mouth when you snap it.

The Goddess Erú turned to the healer. "Titania will be so relieved," she said. "I will give this crown back to her myself." The healer understood, for such mischievous creatures fairies are, how else is the Queen supposed to keep control and power over them with nothing to charm them but her own personality?

The healer bowed and Erú glanced at Andrew. "He must make an offering to them," she said, "to free him from any contracts he has gotten involved with. It has been messy with them, with him. He needs to be free."

The healer nodded in agreement. "I'll take care of it," she said.

"Thank you for your good work," said Erú. She bent down and kissed the healer on the lips, and the healer went into an ecstatic bliss, all of her energy centres opened like flowers to the sun, and when she opened her eyes, Erú was gone.

After a moment, the healer turned to her guides. "Thank you," she said to them, and they nodded their heads and went back to where they had come from. The healer sat back down into her chair and waited for Andrew to open his eyes.

"It's all looked after now; it is finished," she said as soon as he was able to hear and understand her. Andrew sat up tall suddenly in his chair. He was disoriented. He felt as if he had been on a very long journey but didn't know where he had gone to. His body was tense, waiting for a poke or a prod or a hair to be pulled.

"They're gone," said the healer. "They are gone now, and you are safe."

Andrew started to cry, big heavy sobs of relief. "So I wasn't going crazy?" he asked between blubs and sneezing and blowing his nose.

"Not one bit of it" said the healer "for those who think these things are not real, they are the crazy ones".

Andrew really didn't agree with her but he also had not felt a prod or a poke for several minutes, so he chose, at this moment, to believe that she was correct and that whatever it was that had upset him had been removed.

When he had calmed down and after two further glasses of water, the healer said, "Now, there is something that you must do to seal this work true."

"Okay," said Andrew looking at her with wide eyes, paying attention.

"You must buy some chocolate and some Irish whiskey and go to a particular tree in a forest, break up the chocolate and open the cap of the bottle (a small bottle will do), and read out this prayer." The healer wrote down some words on a page for

Andrew and passed it over to him. He looked at it and nodded.

"It is important that you do this soon and that you mean the words when you say them, not just reading them because I told you to read them."

"How will I know which tree it is?" asked Andrew.

"You will know it by how you feel when you see it. Trust your instincts." He paid her what he owed her and said thank and shook her hand, then changed his mind and hugged her. She smiled and showed him to her door. Outside sat a woman who was shivering, waiting for her appointment with the healer.

Andrew looked at his brand new watch, which he had bought with money he won on another bet, this time with greyhounds, and he didn't tell anyone about his winnings. He realised that he had been with her for only one hour.

"I'll be with you in a moment," the healer said kindly to the woman who looked quite upset. Looking back at Andrew and noticing his shiny watch, she said, "Don't forget to make the offering. It's very important." She smiled kindly at him. "It will be okay now; it will all be okay".

Andrew nodded to her, the door closed, and the woman who was waiting looked up questioningly at Andrew.

"She's good," he said, trying to reassure her before he walked away.

As Andrew strode towards his flat, he noticed how tense his shoulders and neck were. With every step he was holding his breath waiting for something or someone to tap him or push him or pull his hair. But nothing happened. He started to relax a little bit, and as he got to his flat, he kept on walking. He walked for an hour and then for another hour, and after the second hour, he really began to feel better.

He found himself at a shop that was just about to close so he went in and found the best bar of chocolate that they had and a small bottle of Irish Whiskey. He put them into his pocket and walked all the way back to his flat. He had a hot bath and some toast and tea and went to bed and slept all the way through the night. It was the best sleep he had had in over two years.

The next day was a Saturday. He called over to his parents' house and borrowed their car and drove to the forest where he went when he was a little boy. He didn't know why he chose that forest in particular, but it just felt like the right place to be. It was a bright crisp Autumn day, and he could feel the leaves crunching under his feet and the sunshine warm on his face as he went deeper and deeper in. And there it was, he knew it because his heart leapt and his stomach said "Yes".

This was the tree where he had been when he was three. Andrew didn't know this, of course, as he was only three at the time, but his heart knew it, for it was the source of all of the troubles. And the adventures. And the learning and the growth. And the peace of mind that he was now experiencing. And for this his heart was very, very thankful. Above all, he now respected the healer, and felt it was important to do what she said and so be totally free.

Andrew opened the whiskey and placed the bottle down at the bottom of the tree. He put the cap of it into his pocket. He then opened up the chocolate bar, broke it into chunks and placed it on the leaves beside the bottle at the base of the tree. He put the crumpled up wrapper into his pocket and pulled out the note from the healer from his wallet. He wasn't happy about leaving the glass bottle of whiskey, and wondered about littering, then he heard a voice in his ear say,

"Pour some of it into the crevice of that stone, right there, and then take the bottle back with you." Andrew jumped, and then he heard tinkles and giggles, and then he laughed along with them. For he was free now and he felt it and knew it and believed everything was finally going to be okay again.

He read out the prayer, the contents of which are between the healer and Andrew and the Fairies. He added a few lines of his own: he pledged to be a better person, to appreciate everything around him, and to plant a tree somewhere where a tree was needed. Then he did a strange thing that took him by surprise. He got down on his knees and kissed the roots of the tree. And he liked it. Feeling the earth beneath him, he also felt the tree soften towards him and his heart opened. He felt nice. He felt good. He felt damn good in fact. Maybe he'd give Grace a call and tell her all about it.

Tribute To Roethke
by way of explanation

What does what it should do needs nothing more
moving slowly towards desire
we come to something without knowing why
how can I dream except beyond this life?

Beautiful my desire and the place of my desire
I was queen of the vale for a short while
living all my hearts summer
running through high grasses

Faced with my own immensity I
woke all the waves and their loose wandering fire
and then I ran
ran ahead of myself
across a field into a little wood
and there I stayed
until the day burned down

Too much reality can be a dazzle
too close immediacy an exhaustion

What lover keeps his song?
I sigh before I sing
I love because I am

I dare caress the stones, the field, my friend
I bare a wound and dare myself to bleed
I think a bird and it begins to fly

I see you, love, I see you in a dream
I hear a noise of bees, a trellis hum
and that slow humming rising into song

A light wind rises and
I become the wind
this shaking keeps me steady
what falls away is always. And near.
If the wind means me
I'm here

A Prayer For Soul Retrieval

I call my spirit back,
I hereby call back my lost power.
I call my spirit back from the anger, abuses and chaos that harmed me.
I hereby call my power back from the people and situations that caused me to lose power and cell tissue.
I call it back.
I call my spirit back into present time.
When I'm in the now, I'm in the everything.
God is in everything, everything is in God, God is in me.

Amen

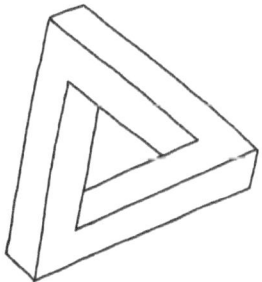

Quilt

You wear a patchwork quilt of all the truths and the lies that you have ever told in your lifetime
All the deeds that you have done are visible in colour and thread and quality of weaving
The lightness truth, the darkness heavy.

The weight of your Soul dependant on your actions and purity
You wear this quilt until the day you die where it is examined
And decisions are made.

Who Am I?

Essence of light I am soul spirit woman medicine woman warrior woman child of Pachamama Mother Earth I walk barefoot in the jungle all senses vibrant alert and ready for danger I am alive I am my breath my body the food that I eat and the dreams that consume me

Who am I?

Motherwoman children of my womb my body is your body but your souls are your own I shall feed nourish protect keep you from harm I'll kill on your behalf I hold you so close to me and then I let you go I see you in everyone and everyone is my sister my brother a child of Pachamama

Who am I?

Man's woman loverspirit graceful floating essence of light I love deeply from dark places I can make you happy if you come to me I'm not afraid to stand beside you to show you all of me to fly in ecstasy so deep my love springs from my heart tapped into the strength of Pachamama helps me change my shape to keep you near me but I will never ask you to change

Who am I?

Cityspiritwoman working woman nature in a lookingglass I'll battle traffic management government to protect my own ones I'll sacrifice pieces of myself here if I have to moderncity spirit woman my desk surrounded by plants and life and pictures of my children reminders of the reasons why

Who am I?

I am the places of my childhood the memories of dreamtimes the salt of the sea the smells in the kitchen the blackness of earth the colours of sadness I am all the music in the world the words both said and left unsaid the moment between sunrise and sunset

I am the union of my parents communion with my loved ones a child of Pachamama the essence of spirit the breath in my body the flesh the marrow the blood and the bone, I am all of it and none of it

I am my breath

Intention To Heal

First I must put my house in order.

And only then can I stand fixed and firm to this present moment
Like a rock to the shore.

I call out to the vastness of the Universe
across all space and time
My voice louder than the Roughness Of Seas
The howling of the wind cannot drown me out
for the certainty of whence I stand
and the truth of my voice
is all that I have.

I call for my Soul pieces
the pieces of my Soul
come back to me right
now from wherever you are
cleansed and healed
and conjoin with me
and make me whole again.

And now I wait.

Always Here Be Magic

I shrink
and sprout my fairy wings
dancing around to get the wherewithal and then
I fly, up up up
to the bough
look down, scan the land below
and dive
heart leaping into mouth
I see my reflection in the pond
as I pull up and skim it
to slow and land on lillypad
on sunless day
clouds pass, grey day, but always magic here
always here be magic

I was driving home and the sky opened a crack and
all this light poured into it from the heavens

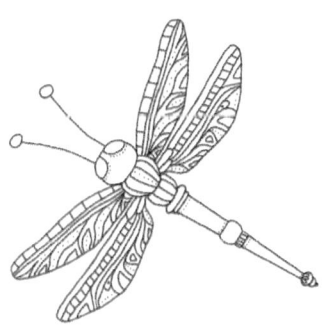

The Rescue

The old woman rocked slowly back and forth in her chair in the living room of her care home. Her eyes were closed. She was muttering to herself words that could be in any foreign language. She had wrinkles etched deeply into her face, behind her eyes, around her mouth and nose. She had seen many things in her life and she was ready to move on. Her walker was beside her, a shaft of sunlight catching it from the nearby window creating a shine on the wall. She wore black, had always worn black. Nobody ever questioned it although her granddaughter bought her a turquoise scarf for her birthday. She secretly loved it; it was her prized possession. As she rocked, she dozed. In and out of this world and that, hardly noticing who was in the room. The carers brought her dinner plate and more often than not it was hardly touched. The woman slept. She did not dream.

Salufia was standing on a rock, a steep one, in the hot blazing suns. She was young, about 30 or so, wearing combat pants and a cut off tee shirt. She had binoculars trained on the incoming storm. "Damnit it wasn't meant to come until next fortnight. It's a sneaky bastard of a thing. If we run evacuation protocols right away, we might just make it."

"But the ships aren't fuelled up yet," said someone beside her, younger than her, male, wearing a similar outfit.

"I realise that," she said curtly, "but it's coming closer and we have no time to lose. This is the one we have been waiting for. It's time. Tell them to take the fuel lead out and prepare for launch. Evacuation protocol 6B."

The man suddenly became alert. "Yes Ma'am," he said, turned and saluted her, and ran in the direction of the docking bay.

"We have no time to lose," she thought to herself. "Alvera!" she shouted down to the woman below. "Sound the siren. It's time." A woman at the base of the mountain also in a similar outfit saluted and ran.

"Nerves of steel, remember? Nerves. Of. Steel," Salufia shouted out after her.

A large drone of a siren thundered out overhead with an automated genderless voice on a loudspeaker breaking through.

"Evacuation has begun. Protocol 6B. Please make your way calmly to your meeting point. You will be received there and ushered to the gate. Bring only what is necessary. This is not a drill."

The droning noise continued, it seemed to gnaw directly at the stomach, it was at the unpleasant frequency of impending doom. Everybody knew what it meant. They had been waiting for this moment for several years. Now that it had actually arrived, many people couldn't believe it was real. But soon the anxiety passed and the people, who had been well trained, went into evacuation mode, briskly gathering their families and essentials and went to their assigned meeting points.

Nobody knew where the ships were, they had been hidden specifically so that people wouldn't interfere with the supply chain. Evacuation was Salufia's expert job. She was good at organising things, particularly in difficult times. People would bend to her and she knew how to squeeze them. She had organised 15 civilian transports and enough supplies for 3 million people for 13 months, just long enough to find somewhere else to refuel. She had done this before, with help, but after the incident on Floriba 10 when she demanded it, they gave her full control over decision making. She was highly recommended by the Federation, and Salufia was quietly confident she could get everyone out this time. She wouldn't have taken the job otherwise. She knew she could do this in her sleep, so she felt well prepared; however, she was also not naïve enough to take things for granted. There was always the possibility of something going wrong. She raised her telescopic eye and looked at the storm once more. It was accelerating; if it kept this trajectory she would only have four hours to get everybody out. That was a tall order but she would do it.

The old woman turned in her chair and her hand slipped to one side, knocking over her china cup which was filled with lukewarm tea. She didn't notice. A carer came over and mopped up the spill; the old woman didn't stir.

It was getting darker. "Get the mandrills!" shouted Salufia, grabbing her gun and ratchet and running out into the public area. People were starting to panic as the storm debris was becoming visible by eye. This was the stuff of nightmares, many people had never seen a real Elerial storm before. Thankfully most of them were managing to hold it together, yet she could feel their fear rising. She stood on the balustrade and spoke into her megaphone:

"You can do this. Stay calm. We still have time but this is not a drill. Do not go back to your residence unless you've left a child there. Everyone must be accounted for. Make your way to the meeting point briskly, now, please, everyone."

The people seemed to calm slightly. With her strength and reputation behind her, they were reassured she was in control. They continued moving with more determination. There was a beeping on the radio strapped to Salufia's thigh:

"Report," she said into it.

"All going to plan here in section 8," said a female voice.

"Good. Any word on that fuel?"

"No Ma'am, but Derivida is working on that now."

Salufia nodded. "Good. Load the backup barrels if he doesn't have time to fill all the tanks. We can figure it out once we are away from here. Keep everyone moving. Check in with Manson every 10 minutes. Time is passing quicker than we realise. We only have 196 minutes until impact, and we want to be loaded and up in the air with at least 10 minutes to spare."

"Yes Mam."

There was a squealing from the crowd, Somebody had fallen over, hands grabbing, pulling, reaching, supporting, back on their feet and marching onwards to the meeting area. It was always better when the crowds were supportive. Salufia pushed away a flashback from Zebron 15, where the crowds were not so helpful to one another. She was still haunted by the look on that girl's face....

"Focus focus," she said to herself, running faster towards the docking bay. "Release the hundreds to save the millions."

Manson was disconnecting the blocks and running the rigs to shut down the star shield. He nodded to Salufia:

"Ready for loading, shields down, all ships fuelled up, loaded and ready for take-off."

The bay doors opened and the people quickly filtered in and went to their designated boarding zones.

"This is going so smoothly, it's almost too good to be true," thought Salufia. Holding the loudspeaker to her mouth and addressing the crowd: "I have done this over 100 times and we had plenty of time to prepare. Let's keep the flow smooth people – make your way to your designated ship. It is time to board now."

People filtered onto the ships, brand new ships and transporters that were practically ancient but still space worthy. Salufia had to do some real hunting to gather so many of them. Going up old style gangplanks on any other day would have been a novelty that the people would really have enjoyed, but there was no time for laughter. Ushers kept the flow of people moving. Salufia clipped on a hoverbelt and elevated to the viewing platform. Yes, everything was in order. She almost had time to phone her mom, she thought. No, she could not be factious. Every little detail was vital. She scanned the bays and spotted something strange.

"This new technology makes it so much easier," she thought. She zoomed in on section 9 and saw one of the technicians dealing with a loose flow pipe. "He's got this," she thought as she checked her PED to look at the storm progress once more. Pressing the com button, she spoke into the mic:

"Pick up the pace people. Mount those steps, get into the ships, go to your cabins as fast as you are able. We still have 10 ships to load and the storm is coming in 164 minutes and counting."

Evening was closing in and the old woman still hadn't woken up. The common room was emptying out as dinner was being served in the dining hall. She wouldn't be going there tonight. Although asleep, her face was tense, as if she was focused on something extremely important. Her lips quivvered; her eyes were moving behind closed eyelids.

Salufia caught sight of Alvera running in with a panicked look on her face. She lowered herself down to ground level and met her.

"The blasted Scorbs are coming!!" Alvera was breathless. "They must have found out about the evacuation ships – what are we going to do? They can't come with us. There's no room and they look ready for a fight."

"Don't worry, I'll take care of it".

Salufia had a backup plan in case this happened. There was a spare ship and some supplies waiting in Zone 41. She revved up her hover and sped out of the docking bay to hunt for the Scorbs. These rebels were dangerous. They were the cause of the 342u uprising, violent to the bone and not to be trusted. She saw them in the distance and was just about able to pick out their leader with her telescopic eye. She drove over the terrain to confront them. Just her, on her own. All she had was a small A45 to protect her, but she wasn't afraid. What she was doing was bigger than they. She had her reputation behind her and she had no time to waste.

She met them whilst in mid-air, but she did not land to stand as an equal. She broke protocol and reached for her loudspeaker to speak from where she hovered. The Scorbs stopped, a real rag-tag bunch. Salufia shivered at the sight of them. Their pack leader beckoned for his people to stop. It was a knife-edge moment, and he knew she had the upper hand. She looked at his face and then started shaking.

"Artemis?" she said into the loudspeaker. She had not seen Artemis in 20 years. He looked the same, much older, but it was still him. He jolted.

"Nobody has called me that in over 20 years," he said, raising his eyes to look at her face. He broke into the biggest smile: "Salu? Is that you?"

Joy and hope filled her body, ecstatic bliss at seeing her lover again after all this time, and she briefly forgot her mission. It was as if their spirits, recognising each other, conjoined and swirled and danced together outside of their bodies, and all they could do was bear witness. But time was ticking and she felt the urgency of her cause snap her back to the moment.

"Please help me," she whispered and something stronger than their reunion pushed her back into her body quickly. "Yes, it's me." She coughed, got her balance and continued.

"I have made arrangements for your people. I expected the Scorbs would come try to sabotage our evacuation, so I thought I would beat you to it." In a lower voice she added "I didn't know you were their leader, Artemis."

"Always for the greater good," said Artemis with a hypnotising smile. "You were always an inspiration to me."

Salufia pulled herself out of his enrapture and continued speaking through the loudspeaker addressing all of the Scorbs: "I have prepared a ship and enough supplies for 800 people for 2 years. It is in Zone 41. You will have to make your way there yourselves. I assume you have pilots able to steer a Zetgack ship?"

Artemis's eyebrows raised and he looked thoughtful, then relieved. "Yes, we do," said Artemis. "How thoughtful of you. And we will accept your kindness." There was a groan from the people surrounding him.

"No raiding or killing is necessary," Artemis spoke to his people. "We are all in the same danger, and we do not have time for bloody violence." He turned to Salufia. "We can now evacuate this planet because of you, and we thank you." He bowed to the ground. "Come with us?" He winked. "We have unfinished business you and I...."

Salufia blushed. "I'll think about it," she said. "I've got to go. Everything you need is in Zone 41, due north of here. Know it?" The Scorbs muttered amongst themselves, and Artemis nodded and saluted her.

In a soft voice directed only at him, Salufia said, "You may see me later. Good luck."

The nurses fussed around the old woman as they laid her on her bed in her private room. They had undressed her, washed her and put on her nightdress, which had little cherries on it. They covered her with her duvet, all the while tut-tutting and tisk-tisking. "She's got to eat something," said one to the other. "It's been three days now." The nurse shook her head. "Should we phone her daughter?" The old woman was in a very deep sleep when the nurses turned off the light and left the room. She turned and a small droplet of saliva dripped onto her pillow.

Salufia checked her time device. Storm approach was down to 35 minutes now. Most of the population had boarded the fleet, children crying as their pets had had to be exterminated. It broke her heart to see them cry, but there was no other choice. The food had to be rationed out, and they didn't have enough to cater for non-essential luxury animals although she had a feeling there was more than one nifter snuck into the ships in random pockets of children, and she hoped she was right. It's important to have the little comforts, particularly in disastrous times.

The ships had already started taking off. Salufia felt a great sense of achievement as she watched the first five ships lift up into space and power off to their designated meeting point. Everything was working on schedule, and she had most certainly earned her two million Cubiks. She went to Alvera to sign off.

"How is it going at your end, President Alvera?" she asked.

"Yes, it's smooth. We couldn't be happier even with these unexpected circumstances. Nice trick with the Scorbs."

Salufia smiled. "News travels fast," she said.

Alvera opened her PED and pressed a few buttons. "Transferring the money now. We the people of Dorphia 6 are forever grateful." They shook hands, then hugged, and President Alvera boarded the diplomatic ship.

Salufia stayed to watch the last of the transporter ships leave. She needed to have complete closure. Once they left, she briskly walked to her own ship. She was free now but she had to leave too. Storm due in 13 minutes. She boarded and quickly shot out of the dock and up and over the planet to observe the Elerial storm hit the weak part of the planet's plate tectonics. And that was that. When would people ever learn? No amount of drilling was ever a good thing. It broke her heart to see the planet rendered lifeless. It was a reminder to her of the fragility of things and that even planets can be destroyed. She tried not to feel the pain of the devastation that ensued below. She knew, even though her mission was the last of the evacuations, that there would still be fatalities; there were always people left behind – how could there not be? But she also knew that most of the people survived because of her. Another job well done. But she felt nothing. No joy, no elation, just a dullness inside, a sense of completeness but also an emptiness.

The radio phone on her dash started blinking. She jumped and then pressed it and saw Artemis's face appearing on her screen. She went from empty to full in a nanosecond.

"I want to thank you on behalf of my people," he said, winking at her again.

"Gratitude accepted," she said, heart leaping to see him up close. Yes, he was still himself, still so very attractive to her.

"Where are you headed?" He asked.

"Wasn't sure yet. This is my 111th evac. I've been asked to Morag 12 to help them, but I'm feeling I need to take a break for a while – like a long break."

"We're heading to Glaceon 7. There's a colony there that invited us to train them. They plan to overthrow the civilisation. It's always nice to share our skills, and after the way you treated us, as real people, some of my people are already talking about settling down and wanting to be part of something bigger."

"How did you end up here? And leading such a violent bunch of people?"

"Hey, we are not all bad. It's been a while. I have so many stories, bet you do too. Why don't you join me? For a while anyway? Come get to know me again. I promise we won't bite, and maybe you'll have something you could teach us too. Teach me?" He cocked his head to one side, and she melted.

"Glaceon 7, eh?"

"North face, section 134.321"

"Maybe I'll see you there. Over and out." Salufia smiled.

The screen darkened as her little ship continued on its elevation with Dorphia 6 dissolving beneath her. It didn't take her long to decide what she wanted to do next. She set her coordinates to Glaceon 7 and hit the hyperdrive. She could always change her mind.

The old woman smiled in her sleep. Her work here was done. She took her final breath and slipped out of her body. Looking down at Juliet on the bed, earth bound, shrivelled and old and wracked with arthritis and dementia, she knew it was time for the next adventure. Juliet had served her well. She didn't need to grieve. A new life beckoned on Glaceon 7 with one of the most interesting and exciting beings she had ever met in all of her lifetimes. She didn't want to miss a moment of this. Time to go and have some fun for a change.

Mission Almost Impossible

I was chosen for this mission
I accepted, but no handbook was given
and when I was born into it
I forgot everything

I had to learn it all from scratch
I thought I was an ordinary child
my will entraining many indicators to blink in tandem
went unnoticed

Staring out the window at night waiting for the fairies
to bring me back to my real family
No scraps of clues were given, no post-it notes, threads or tacks
adorned my bedroom wall

Only time unfolded the map within,
sacred time, chronological time, years passing by
some slow, some quick
whilst I grew into myself

Passion to change the world and urgency to leave a legacy behind
transformed
Shedding of friends, outgrowing of places and things
simplifying attachments and expectations

The alchemy of madness into deep stillness

No need for having
I belong to me now
And my mission is complete

A Prayer Of Gratitude

Dear God,

Thank you thank you

Quench

And now I am free
of my own chains of
obligation rank and king
to claim sovereignty to no one
but the sky, the earth beneath my feet

I walk with giants and remember
who I am
at one with all beings
and yet I still taste
someone else's cigarette smoke in my nostrils
hear someone else's baby laughing
and am thrust into someone's yet again intrusion as
she speaks
to her doctor on the telephone
so for myself I must claim
the sunniest spot on the veranda
the best slice of cake and
the flag on the mountaintop

I claim ... what?
this? the illusion they've been
speaking of all my life?
what rights have I in this reality?
what claim and who am I to make it when
children suffer...
grown children suffer...?

And is it true they're following me around

or are we all just
going in the same direction?

Does moon follow sun
follow moon or is it
all projections on a screen
and we're the shadows projected
in-between?

For what reason does that baby cry?
The futility of it all? Or the
safe warm space where
no decisions need be made?

Nature is the only thing that is
not afraid of death or change
beneath the layers of dank soil
the earthworm spins its merry nest
never worrying about
the cost of its next meal
and back to me – yes
close your eyes, feel the sun on your face

s
t
i
l
l
n
e
s
s

o
f

m
i
n
d

And I disappear once more
into myself

I am but a channel
an empty tray upon which
to place some glasses and
serve yourself, so drink,
drink from me child
for if this life is suffering at the heart of it
then at the very least,
you can quench your thirst

Growing Up

I must unpeel myself from your bones
pluck myself out of your eyes and your ears
and set you free.

You're no longer a child
and have no need of such a fierce protector.

But the world is such a harsh place my love,
I struggle with letting you go forth in it alone.

Song Of Woman 3

I am woman
and I love

Endless capacity for love and pain
endless need
for love
and pain

Loss of focus
dual imagery
parallax
of loss

Oh Scarlet Heart if only you were not so demanding

I am woman
stronger now and more deeply
connected
to all things living or once lived

A conduit
for words already spoken
nothing needs be left unsaid

Live through me
flow through me
breathe
cry
be

I am woman
I cherish my inner child
I put my arms around her
and love her
and who she turned out to be

I transformed my pain
because it's mine

I am woman
silver hair, no longer in demand
I do not bleed
not wanted by any man

This frees me up
to birth myself
The pain of birth
as pure as truth

Gaping hole
needs to be filled
I fill myself whole

Dancing
under
moonlight
with
black
cat

Behold the old man in the chair
his glasses slipping down his nose

as he snores himself into yet another dream

Other women
talking secrets
in circle
sacred wholeness
standing taller
in flat shoes

So fly away now
go now
leave me here
I am fine

I cut the silver threads connected from
my heart to your wings
and unfold my own
outstretched and soaring

We live the way we die
and die the way we live
we fly

In Stillness

Somewhere behind the noise lies the silence
a lake of stillness
I dive in there

But alas I am fished out by distractions
each time I dip my melancholy toes into it I feel
more at peace
This time I stare at my own reflection, peering
deeper into the lagoon each time
I can almost taste myself

Plunging in I hold my breath
time stops
only my heartbeat and this silence
softness
observance
just beingness
just be
this

The longer I can stay in here
the more I feel alive

Flowers, raindrops, crickets, mountains
all inside of me when I am deep within the lake
the womb of earth
Just floating, being

panning out and see the many others who have not made it yet

See this golden earth then
pan further out
and you can see this golden earth inside a raindrop reflection
on a blade of grass on another planet
where some being who was as distressed as I once was
is looking for a way to dissolve herself into this stream
where all becomes one

Maybe The World Isn't Broken

Maybe it is just our perception that tells us there is an imbalance
Maybe it is our eyes that follow what it is that they follow
magnetised to our deepest desires

Do they follow the pack
or the dark
or the light
what do you prefer?

Maybe the world is supposed to be a beautiful hostile environment
Lion was created to devour antelope,
crocodile created to snap up unsuspecting fish -
are you a shark or a minnow?

There are human predators and human prey too my love,
a frog does not get to decide what it is, but we humans do.
We are bountiful in that we can choose our next move based on our experiences,
we are not always a knee jerk reaction

If you heal your inner wounds you are less likely to be triggered,
less likely to prey off of others for short term satisfaction,

more likely to follow the path of light....

but a scorpion knows only what a scorpion knows best
and a spider is lost without the fly in her nest
and a cat will never tell you its name no matter how often you plead her or feed her

Some mysteries will remain intact
we choose what we choose
and we wear those choices in the fabric of our Soul

Elixir Transformangelico

Martin wore a brown suit. He carried a brown briefcase, leather, worn on one side with a tear on the handle. He lived alone; on weekdays his alarm was set for 7am. He ate muesli for breakfast and took the metro to work. He had been in the same job for 11 years as a data analyst for a large pharmaceutical company. He was always on time, always checked off his "to do" list, had his coffee at 11am, smiled at the receptionist and brought a packed lunch.

On the weekends Martin went to the history museum or the cinema, he walked in the park and he wrote down his thoughts in a journal. They were every day, ordinary thoughts, but he wrote them down nonetheless as it seemed like the thing to do. He had brown wallpaper, no artwork on his walls, no pets. Martin wasn't unhappy, but he wasn't happy either. Life went on at an even keel, which suited him fine. Until Suzanna.

Suzanna was flamboyant, she had 33 different colourful scarves all with bright designs, gradients and flowers on them. She laughed out loud, she waved her hands about when she got excited, which was often, and she got a job in Martin's company. She was given the desk next to Martin. Martin was quite put out by this. Suzanna would have long loud conversations on the telephone, she draped herself over the chair and chewed on the end of a pencil while dangling her foot back and forth, her Mary Jane shoe dangling on the edge of her foot as if it couldn't quite decide whether it was going to fall off or stay on. Martin sometimes caught himself wondering too and had to pull himself away and back to his work. When Suzanna was at her desk Martin often found himself experiencing a terrible crawling sensation in his left shoulder. It wasn't quite an itching; it was stronger and harsher than that, deep in his muscles. It seemed to spread itself across his back and down into his hips and legs. It became at times unbearable. He couldn't sit still; he had to get up and walk about. He sometimes found himself wringing his hands while walking back and forth as he tried to get the awful itchy crawly jumpy feeling to subside.

Suzanna often asked Martin if she could get him anything from the canteen. She asked him if he was okay when she noticed his wringing hands, but he didn't like to talk to her. She was, to all intents and purposes, a nice person, and Martin tried his best to like her, but ultimately every time she showed up to work, which was often late, he would get a sinking feeling. This feeling was also new to Martin. But he grinned and bore it and kept going.

One day about 3 weeks after her first day, Suzanna received a phone call from the hospital. She froze, which was very unusual for her, and Martin couldn't help noticing. She nodded her head in response to the voice on the phone, put the phone down and whispered to Martin,

"My mother has taken ill. She's in St James's. I have to go." She wrapped her scarf around her shoulders and walked out of the office, assumedly on her way to the hospital.

Martin was torn between the relief of not having her presence next to him and concern for her and for her mother. He shook it off and turned back to his computer. But he noticed out of the corner of his eye that she had left her wallet on the desk. He stood up to see if she was still in the office, but she had already left. He eyed the wallet, looked at his watch, and noticed another new feeling opening up inside him. He couldn't name it, it felt jumpy but not crawly, fast, light inside him like fresh air hitting your face when you open the window in winter. All of these new feelings around Suzanna were quite upsetting, but he thought about how nice she was to him and how upset she must be about her mother and then how upset again she would be when she looked inside her bag and couldn't find her wallet. He decided to go after her. He checked that he had his own wallet and keys, just in case, and then he walked smartly with the wallet in his hand, leaving his coat on the hook so that it would look like he was still in the building.

When he got outside into the fresh air, he looked around him to see if he could see her. Wait – there was a woman with an orange and pink scarf bobbing down at the end of the road – that must be her. He ran after her, looking both ways at the intersection, and saw her cross the road in the distance. Yes, it definitely was her as she was wearing a red dress and green shoes, with an orange scarf. What a combination! Martin was focused on catching up with her, so he moved swiftly, dodging the street vendors, not realising that St James Hospital was in the opposite direction.

She turned another corner, he ran to catch up with her. He saw her stop outside what seemed to be some sort of church. It had three steps up to a large door, which was in a gothic style, painted a creamy yellow. He stopped, breathless; it now becoming obvious to him that she wasn't going to a hospital at all. She turned to him and smiled as if she was expecting him. His heart seemed to leap into his mouth as he approached her.

"You left your wallet," he said between breaths, holding it out to her.

"Thank you, Martin. I was hoping you'd see that," she smiled and took the wallet from him, tucking it into her handbag.

Puzzled, he cocked his head to one side like a puppy.

"Come with me?" she asked

"Is your mother sick at all?" he questioned.

"She's here, come see, I'm sure she would love to meet you."

He fought the urge to look at his watch. He anticipated the itching sensation, but for once, his curiosity got the better of him.

"Why not," he said. She opened the door.

They both stepped inside and the door closed itself behind them. Her shoes made a tick-tack sound on the marble floor as she walked up the corridor. Martin followed her. They went into a very grand room, something out of Victorian England. Martin's eyes widened as he noticed antique furniture perfectly preserved, pristine in fact. One large sofa, a coffee table, a dark portrait on the wall and a mahogany cabinet. He wandered over to the large mirror that hung over a mantelpiece and ran his hand along its frame. Gold leaf, circa 1857.

"Impressive," he thought.

"What is this place?"

"A very well kept secret," she replied, walking over to a mahogany cabinet that had upon it a sliver tray, a dusty bottle of some sort of liquid and two small glasses. She opened the bottle and poured a thimbleful of liquid into each glass, then gestured to the chairs.

"Sit".

Martin sat, quite out of his comfort zone. She handed him a glass, toasted it and sat down beside him on the sofa, kicking off her shoes and lying back on the pillows, making herself comfortable.

"To Mama," she said and knocked hers back. Martin drank his too in one gulp, placing the glass beside hers on the coffee table. The liquid was viscous and sweet, like honey, but with some sort of spice in it. He had never tasted anything like this before. It warmed his stomach almost immediately; he decided that he liked it. The room seemed to swim before him, he fell deeper into the chair and closed his eyes.

He found himself in a large white room, like the ones they have in art museums, only there was no artwork. There was an old woman painting something on the floor.

"She brought you to see me," the woman said in a crackly voice. "Good." Martin didn't know what to say, it took him a moment to realise that she was actually talking to him. He said nothing.

"Look," said the woman gesturing down to the floor. She was painting blues and greens, white and pinks. Martin looked and felt happiness flood into his body. It was overwhelming. He felt like he lost his balance, but he regained it quickly enough. Then he looked again, deeper this time. He recognised something in the image, but it seemed out of reach.

"Don't look with your eyes," said the woman. "Look with your heart."

"How?"

The woman reached out and tapped him on his chest three times. "That should help," she said.

Martin felt something in his chest burst open, like a firework. This really was most uncomfortable.

The pain subsided as he wondered how he had gotten into this situation at all.

"Look at the painting," the old woman said. His eyes were drawn back in, and all of a sudden he could see himself as a boy, laughing, running on the hilltop with a little white dog – Sparky! It was Sparky! Ooh how he missed Sparky! After he was hit by that car, his parents didn't buy him another pet. It truly was delightful to see him again. Martin smiled. The woman continued to paint.

The images faded and he saw the colours again, so he followed her trail to another spot of colour, swirls of oranges and greens, with some greys creeping in. He peered into the colours but could see only colours. He looked at the old woman and she smiled, tapped his heart three times and he jolted. The firework didn't go off this time; it was just a warming sensation.

Martin looked into the colours beneath him and saw himself at 13, crying on his bed, heartbroken. His mother had died. There were yellow flowers in the hallway. It was as if he was experiencing that moment again, the very painful realisation that his mother would never kiss him goodnight ever again. It still hurt. He pulled away from the memory and looked at the old woman, a tear forming in his eye.

"Hurts still, doesn't it?" she said to him.

He nodded, and the tear ran down his cheek.

"Look here," she said, pointing to another section of her painting where all it seemed to be was swirls of reds, oranges and yellows. He squinted his eyes and then remembered it wasn't his eyes that saw, before he could ask himself if he really wanted to do this again.

He took a breath, tapped his own heart three times and the images came into focus. There he was with Mary, the love of his life, the girl he met in college.

"Beautiful, wasn't she?" asked the old woman. Martin nodded, once more feeling something moving in his heart as he looked at a younger version of himself with his arm around Mary's shoulder cuddling her close to him, and her cuddling into him. The images swirled and got darker. She was shouting, he was shouting and then he was crying, alone. The images dissolved, and the colours on the floor grew darker -, greys and shades of black - getting softer until they reached a very familiar colour, brown. Just like his wallpaper.

"That's when you shut your heart," said the old woman, putting down her paintbrush and looking at Martin directly. Martin didn't know what to say. He hadn't realised that he had done that. He was just getting on with things.

"My Suzanna really upset your world, didn't she?"

He nodded again with a weariness. He wanted to leave now. He had had enough of this strange woman rubbing his unhappiness into his face.

"You have a choice, you know. You can bring the colours back if you open your heart," said the old woman. "Would you like to see the rest of your painting should you continue the way you are going?"

Martin didn't feel like he had any choice. The old woman continued painting, swirling browns and blacks on the floor, eventually getting darker and darker, until she created a vortex of blacks and then, that was it. Martin was transfixed by the black swirling vortex. He walked over to it as if he was being pulled into it and peered down at the floor. He felt and looked like he was going to jump into it. The woman approached him and put her hand on his back, pulling him back.

Martin eventually managed to speak again. "Are there memories there too, in my future? In your painting?"

"Well it hasn't happened yet for you. These are possibilities more than memories. Your painting could change, depending on what you do with your life now. This painting here, this bit, is like a weather forecast, based on the patterns in your life as they are going forward. But if you change something, do something different, courageous, daring, fun, out of character, flamboyant, anything is possible." She laughed. "A flamboyant gesture could shift your entire future. How do you feel about that?"

Martin felt groggy, like he was going to be sick. He wasn't sure if he had fallen down, but the next thing he knew, he opened his eyes and was alone in the beautiful Victorian room.

Once he got his bearings, he got up, brushed down his suit and saw how brown it was, perhaps for the first time. "My life is so brown that even my clothes are brown," he thought to himself. He looked up and saw his reflection in the mirror on the wall. "Did I dream this? Am I dreaming now?" He was still surrounded by the beautiful pristine furniture, but he was alone. He noticed his glass, exactly where he had placed it on the coffee table, and there was only one glass there. It was as if all trace of Suzanna had disappeared. He walked over to the bottle and saw the label: "Elixir Transformangelico". The rest of it was scratched out.

He picked up the bottle and held it to the light. It was half full, and the light seemed to dance inside the liquid, like little starbursts. He turned it and the little starbursts changed colours. He shrugged his shoulders and put the bottle back down again, looking around him once more as if he would find Suzanna behind the furniture. But she really was not there, so he stepped out of the room and walked slowly down the corridor. The yellow door opened before he got to it. It beckoned him to step outside, so he did, and the door closed behind him.

The city street was busy, bustling, people walking determinedly going someplace, some of them on their phones talking, others texting or reading texts, many of them had take-away coffee cups in their hands. Many people walked with their heads down, looking at the ground. He saw mostly sad faces. It was as if the first time he ever noticed what was going on around him. Everything felt different, more alive, brighter. It was as if he had been living a life in black and white and had just stepped into a brand new world of high definition. It reminded him of the movie, "The Wizard of Oz", when Dorothy arrived in Oz in full colour. Only he didn't think he had gone anywhere. Or perhaps he had been somewhere and came back again. He really was confused.

He saw a bird on the street picking chips out of a container that had been thrown there. "Good for you," he thought. He saw a homeless man in a sleeping bag and, without thinking, reached into his pocket and took out €15. It was all the cash he had on him. He went over to the man and put it into his hand.

"Thank you, sir; blessings on you sir," said the homeless man, smiling in gratitude. Martin felt good about doing that, and as he walked back to the office, he felt lighter in his step.

When he got to his desk, Suzanna's desk was still empty. He wondered where she was and what had happened.

"It's quiet without Suzanna today isn't it," said George as he walked past Martin on his way to the canteen. "It's her first day off since she started. I guess we are getting used to her!" George snickered and went on.

"Day off?" thought Martin. He wanted to slap himself on the head, he really was confused now.

He stood up and went to the bathroom and washed his face. When he came back, he stopped at Suzanne's desk and examined the objects she had there: a little vase with a single flower in it, maybe three days old, a container with paper clips and rubber bands, and a photograph. He picked it up. It was Suzanne and an older woman, taken outdoors in a park somewhere. Both women were smiling. It was a nice photograph. As he looked, he realised that the older woman looked just like the woman who was creating the painting. How was that possible?

Later, after work, Martin decided to take a detour and go back to the building where he had been earlier, with or without Suzanne. He recalled the direction that he went and retraced his steps but he couldn't find the turnoff or the doorway. There was no sign of a similar door anywhere. After traipsing about for almost an hour, he felt defeated and went into the nearest cafe and ordered a hot chocolate with whipped cream and sugar. He sat in the booth and stirred his drink, thinking about the old woman, the painting, the colours on the floor, and what she said to him. How his heart had exploded like a firework; how it felt warm and open right now.

As he finished his hot chocolate, he made a decision. Whether what he saw was real or not didn't matter. What did matter was how he lived his life from this moment forward. He did not want to get sucked into a black vortex. He remembered the old woman saying: "a grand gesture, flamboyant, courageous". He didn't know what that would look like. He knew it would be out of his comfort zone, but he would do it, whatever it was. He paid and left.

The next day was Friday. Martin had overslept, so he missed breakfast and ran to catch his train. He got out two stops early and walked the rest of the way. A pretty scarf in the window of a clothing shop caught his eye. He went inside and bought it and had them gift wrap it. Two shops further on, he saw a plant with red flowers, so he went in and bought that too. He hummed a tune to himself that he had heard on the radio. When he got into the office, he picked out a small blue dish from the canteen, placed it on his desk and put the plant onto it. He put the package on Suzanna's desk and switched on his computer.

She arrived in, 10 minutes late, hung up her coat and noticed the plant on Martin's desk. "I really like your new plant," she said. He smiled. Then she noticed the package. She looked at Martin questioningly.

"I thought you might like it," he said to her.

She opened it and took out the scarf. "Ooh it's very pretty, thank you!" she said, blushing. "I'm going to a party later this evening, would you like to come with me?"

"Yes please," replied Martin.

"Do you own anything that isn't brown? To wear to the party, I mean?" she asked.

"I'm actually not sure," he laughed. "I'll see what I can rustle up."

"Great," she said, replacing the scarf she had been wearing with her new one.

Life was going to be much more colourful from now on, he would make sure of it.

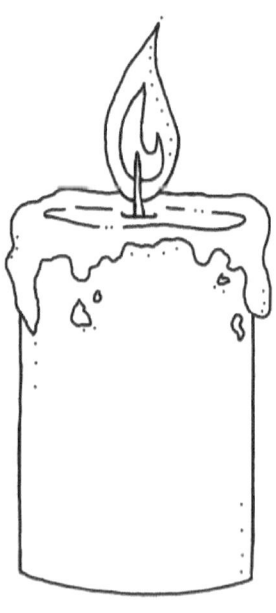

Don't Give Up

You can hold the light, even if you feel alone.
those who want it will fly towards it when they are ready,
those who can't take the brightness,
will try to snuff it out.

Don't despair

Tend to your light, keep it bright and strong.
feed it gently, with love, hope, dreams....
dance in your light, trust it and watch it grow,
expand and know you're not alone.

Keep moving towards the light no matter what

There are many lights dancing in the darkness,
perhaps unaware of each other
spinning and climbing like stars in the night sky
over the rugged cliffs and joints in the landscape

It's time to believe we can make it

What one does makes it easier for others
we are helping each other regardless of geography, geometry
space and time and all dimensions
knitting together the gaps in our Souls
to fill all the spaces with love

Juniper

Hello there! It is so good of you to come to see me. I have been here for what seems like forever. Most people walk past; they don't see me at all. It is so nice to have your attention. Yes, I would like to talk with you. Thank you for asking me. I want nothing from you, but perhaps a few moments of your time. I am not good with time. Time goes so slowly, and then suddenly I realise that it has passed so quickly.

Please, stay here for a while, I want to tell you about my life. I grew up right here at the base of this canyon. It took a long time for me to find my strength as, when I was born, I was very little. For 18 months, I searched for the right place to put down my roots. But once I did, I've been here ever since. Even when the night winds threatened to blow me over, even though the hot days burnt my growing skin, I remained in this place all of my life. My mother and father are far away from me. I never knew them. Thankfully I was a resilient child. Who looked after me, you ask? Well, I depended on the kindness of the land around me to support and nurture me. And although this land is not kind, it provided me with everything that I needed. For that I am forever grateful. And I am still here! Many years later.

How old am I? Why I believe 400 years old, but time is not something that I am clear about. I get muddled. Oh, the things that I have seen. Once these caves were sacred you know. People came, dressed in fine things, banging drums and singing together long into the night. People got married here, they died here and were buried in that canyon over there. There was laughter and love here, anger and hate, all of what you human beings call emotions. So fleeting yet so powerful. Ahh, it was a pleasure to behold. I grew very fond of those peoples. Children came and told me secrets. Adults came and wept beneath my shade. Babies were brought here to be celebrated. But no longer. It is all different now. That was many many years ago, how long I do not know. Time is a difficult concept for me. It is so long since I have been here. In a turn of the moon, a whole season has passed.

 Who do I remember most you ask? Well, let me think ... I do remember a little girl, or was she a woman? She would sit and sing beside me every day just before the morning broke. Oh how I loved her voice. I turned to her one day to thank her, but she was already an old woman. Yes I have been here many many years. Those inscriptions on the canyon walls? No, I have never seen them, for I cannot go inside. I hear many people speaking of them with delight in their voices. Even now they shout out loud like wolves, like coyotes! Wild dogs and people are very alike you know. I see the wild dogs under the moonlight many times as they ravenously search for something to fill their bellies. And I see the people over there, sitting under the shade of the Bedouin tent, drinking coffee and playing their music so loud it sometimes echoes off of the rocks and stones. They are ravenous too but in a different way. I have learned many things in my time here, and people are always the same though their methods of transportation and the clothing they choose to wear may have changed.

It is beautiful here at night, so beautiful. People came on camels, on mules, and stayed outside to look at the stars. Some have slept at my feet, laughing and drinking and singing throughout the night. Now they have these contraptions with wheels – what are they called? So noisy and they stir up much sand, which blows onto me and sits on me for hours. Thankfully mostly they are far away. One time a boy carved something into my skin with a knife, so I have scars.

I don't have anyone to talk to so I don't know the names of things. I hear many different languages being spoken and I listen. There are people who come here with reverence and grace, and people who come to destroy. Such is the nature of humankind, so I have learned, over my 400 years. Ahh yes, I remember someone else! A long long time ago there was a man who came every day. He wore white, and his whole body was covered in white except for his dark brown face and his sand-encrusted eyebrows. He was good to me. He would drink richly from his water skin and then always spared a few drops for me. Very kind. Little did he know I could drink from a whole river beneath the beneath, but he couldn't see the river, oh no. But it was there, and it still is there. It is my life force. Things that you cannot see exist even if you do not know about them. Good things and bad things alike – such things remain buried deeply in the bedrock, like secrets and lies. They will eventually come out my dear; they will eventually be seen. That is my message to you friend. Know that what lies beneath the land influences what is above it. For you can see how beautiful my branches are, how wonderfully green my leaves, for the water here is hidden but it is pure and beautiful. If the people had known about it, they would have already destroyed this mountain, so I will not say anything more.

And you? Where do you drink from my dear? Where is the source of your life force? And is it as pure as my own? How do you know if someone is drinking from clear water, or dirty water filled with lies and hate? You can see it in their eyes. I have seen people of all types and purities as I have seen many things. I may not have eyes like you, but 400 years is a very long time to be alive. Now dear, I am tired, so I will rest a while. And you will probably be gone from here by the time that I wake up. Or perhaps you are going already. Is that the moon? Yes, there is nobody here. I speak once more to myself, the wind the sand and sky. But that is the best company of all, for they never disagree with me.

A Prayer To Open Sacred Space

I call on the four directions, North, South, East and West.
Please bring your presence here and witness us as we set our intention to heal.
Wrap your light around us, share your wisdom with us, teach us how to respect all living beings.

I call upon our Great Mother Earth.
We are here, and we see you in your beauty and your pain.
We honour you and hold you in our hearts,
for the healing that we do for ourselves is also healing you.

I call upon the energies of our ancestors.
Our time is now, and we release you with love and grace,
in huge gratitude for all the burden and pain that you bore. We let those patterns go now as we take our rightful place in space and time to create a new paradigm of love.

I call upon the elements earth, fire, air, water.
Allow us to harness your power.
Help us find the strength that we need to step away from the path of fear.
Help us ground ourselves, let go of emotional pain and reconnect to the fire that burns within.

I call upon the planets, Grandmother Moon and Father Sky.
When we stand beside you, we are no longer small.
Hold us and remind us that we are powerful beings, that power is not good or bad, but it propels us to bring our dreams into form.
Help us see in the dark, to see through the darkness and to remind us that we are made of stars.

I call upon the Angels, the Masters, the Elemental Spirits.
Help us to infuse our hearts, our minds and our Souls with love.
Surround us with light, take away our burdens, disconnect us from pain.
Help us remember that we are never alone.

Great Spirit, you who are known by a thousand names, you who are the unnameable one.
Open our hearts and show us what we need to do, where we need to be, and how we best can serve.
Remind us of the goodness of all beings, the Divine nature of the Soul.
Help ease the burdens in our minds, remove the blocks and open the pathways so we can create a world for all made from a space of love.

With deep gratitude we give thanks that we are here.
We give thanks that that we know who we are.
We give thanks that we know what we have to do.
We are grateful that we have this opportunity to sing the song of life for one more day.

About The Author

Abby Wynne is best known for her self-care books which include the bestselling books Energy Healing Made Easy, The Book of Healing Affirmations, and the One Day at a Time Diary. She has also written what she calls her 'instruction manuals for life' which are composed of How to Be Well (translated into 3 languages), and Heal Your Inner Wounds.

Abby has been writing poetry and stories since she was 6 and recently has begun writing prayers. Stretching outwards to show her full and true voice to the world, Abby has many things to say that cannot be said in one genre of work.

Find out how Abby can help you on your journey to healing via her website www.abby-wynne.com

www.ingramcontent.com/pod-product-compliance
Lightning Source LLC
Chambersburg PA
CBHW021432080526
44588CB00009B/505